# *The Primary Teacher's Survival Guide*

FOR FIRST YEAR TEACHERS

Pamela A. Heyda

Heinemann
Portsmouth, NH

**Heinemann**
A division of Reed Elsevier Inc.
361 Hanover Street
Portsmouth, NH 03801–3912
www.heinemann.com

*Offices and agents throughout the world*

© 2002 by Pamela A. Heyda

**Library of Congress Cataloging-in-Publication Data**
Heyda, Pamela A.
    The primary teacher's survival guide / Pamela A. Heyda.
        p. cm.
Includes bibliographical references and index.
    ISBN 0-325-00401-3 (pbk. : alk. paper)
     1.  First year teachers—United States—Handbooks, manuals, etc.
2. Education, Primary—United States—Handbooks, manuals, etc.
I. Title.
LB2844.1.N4 H49 2002
372.11—dc21                                                    2002005722

*Editor:* Lois Bridges
*Production service:* Colophon
*Production coordinator:* Lynne Reed
*Cover design:* Night & Day Design
*Typesetter:* LeGwin Associates
*Manufacturing:* Jamie Carter

Printed in the United States of America on acid-free paper
06   05   04   03   02   RRD   1   2   3   4   5

For my parents,
Jerome and Jane Heyda,
my greatest teachers.

# Contents

# Acknowledgments

I could not have written this book without the support of some very special people.

Thank you to: The staff of Sunnybrae Elementary School in San Mateo, California, who gave me the encouragement and support I needed to survive my first year of teaching.

To my coworkers Janet Amato, Betty Deeney, and Joanne Orlando for their steadfast friendship, cheerleading, and wisdom.

To April Lee for reading my manuscript in its very early stages and inspiring me to think like a writer.

To Stephen Cary for believing in my ability to write.

To Lois Bridges, my editor at Heinemann, for her guidance, support, and expertise.

And finally to my husband, John Wall, for his brilliant photography, love, and patience, and for taking care of me on the days I was too tired to blink.

# Introduction

The countdown was on. Only six more days to go before my first day of teaching, and I felt ready to start.

I arrived at my school and was greeted warmly by my new principal. As she gave me the grand tour, I immediately felt welcomed, at home, liked, and appreciated. I knew I had found my calling and was thrilled that after a year and a half of substitute teaching and doing all the required credential work, I finally had my own classroom, teaching first grade. I was introduced to many kind and smiling coworkers who offered to help if I needed anything.

I was about to find out that I needed everything!

This is meant to be the book I needed six years ago.

Since my first day I have learned a lot. To a large degree, I *feel* I have been carrying out my vision. I have experienced countless rewards and challenges including moving my classroom five times, working at two schools, and teaching two grade levels. There were critical times when I wished I'd known then what I know now. In moments of reflection I have thought to myself, "We never covered *this* in teacher training!" I also thought, "If I were to help out a new teacher, this is what I'd tell him or her . . . ."

I am thrilled to have the opportunity to share what I've learned over the years. Your first year of teaching doesn't have to be as hard for you as it was for me.

# What Is this Book About?

This book is about my life as a teacher. It is filled with things that I do in the classroom. I am sharing with you the important shortcuts, lessons, and tools-of-the-trade to become an effective teacher and to help make your job a little easier.

## Grade Levels

This book is written for grade levels kindergarten through three. Although my main experience is in grades one and two, I feel much of my teaching is appropriate for all primary grades.

## Questions Posed by New Teachers

Each chapter is titled with a question commonly asked by new teachers. To write them, I referred back to my notes as a student teacher and all the questions and worries I had then. The answers cover all the basic information you need to know as a new teacher.

The chapters are ordered according to what information you need first. For example, before the children arrive you need to set up your classroom. How Do I Set Up My Classroom? is the first chapter. Then you need to know how to survive the first days of school.

## Chapter Summaries

### Chapter 1: How Do I Set Up My Classroom?

Thoughts on desk and furniture arrangement. Creating a circle area. Designing a classroom library and what to consider in its organization. And ideas for simple bulletin boards that can stay up all year and can easily be changed and updated.

### Chapter 2: How Do I Survive the First Days of School?

Tips for meeting and greeting the students when they first walk through the door. Establishing routines such as using the bathroom, getting a drink of water, and lining up. Some ideas for first day activities like touring the classroom and school, reading stories, writing, and creating a self-portrait.

### Chapter 3: How Do I Implement Classroom Management?

Establishing classroom rules, including some sample rules. How to teach the rules. Activities including brainstorming and rule bingo. Creating appropriate and reasonable consequences for breaking the rules, documenting behavior, and implementing classroom management. Tips on consistency. And how to handle difficult students.

### Chapter 4: What Are Some Teaching Strategies and Activities I Can Use?

Using the core curriculum. Developing your own thematic curriculum. Teaching strategies such as setting goals, making a lesson engaging, and modeling. Student activities for all grades, including brainstorming, developing cooperative groups, and worksheets. The timing and content of homework and encouraging its completion.

### Chapter 5: How Do I Stay Organized?

Keeping up with paperwork. Creating an *everything binder*. Organizing the curriculum and filing student work. Establishing routines to become a more efficient teacher.

### Chapter 6: How Do I Prepare for . . . ?

Getting ready for back-to-school night. What to prepare and what to expect. How to set up and conduct parent conferences. How to use student work and test scores to establish report card grades. Preparing for open house and letting your students be the guides. Tips on creating outstanding substitute teacher lesson plans. What to expect and do during the last days of the school year.

### Chapter 7: How Do I Teach and Still Have a Life?

The benefits of being stress free in the classroom. Simple and quick relaxation techniques. Establishing boundaries. Ways to relax during the school day, including creating a Teacher Survival Box. Avoiding illness and maintaining a sense of humor.

### Chapter 8: What Resources Do I Have?

Where to find supplies that are cheap or free. Asking for donations. Receiving help and support from coworkers and other school staff. A list of questions and who can answer them for you.

### Humor Sidebars

Each chapter begins with a *humorous moment* sidebar, a true story of a classroom experience that relates to the chapter question.

### Getting the Most out of This Book

Think of this book as a guide to surviving your first year of teaching. I have written it so that you can use it as an easy reference or sit down and read it all in a night or two. Like any survival guide, it does not contain all the answers. Chapter 8 on resources, helps guide you in the right direction.

### Disclaimer

Of course there are as many ways to teach as there are teachers. The suggestions in this book are things that work for me. Many of the techniques in this book have been handed down by teachers for years and passed on to me. I'm not even sure where many originated. You may want to modify the strategies to fit you and your students' needs. Or you might not agree with something and leave it out altogether. As you journey through your first year of teaching you may even create new techniques and share them with your coworkers.

# How Do I Set Up My Classroom?

**M**y very first day of teaching was less than a week away. I had just gotten my job and was bubbling with anticipation. My classroom was the old staff room! I had been hired at the last minute because the governor had just implemented "class size reduction" in grades 1–3. Schools reducing class sizes to twenty pupils suddenly needed more classrooms. I had heard stories about new teachers setting up their rooms in the auditorium, gymnasium, on the stage, in multi-use rooms, and like me, in the staff rooms. There I was in a small portable classroom—Room 15—with a copy machine, full-size refrigerator, and Coke vending machine. This was definitely not what I had fantasized about in my credential program. I expected a large, cheerful, sunny room filled with little desks and chairs, colorful bulletin boards, cupboards filled with supplies, and shelf after shelf of children's books. Room 15 was not my dream, but I was determined to do everything I could to make it the rich, engaging, and inviting learning environment I had envisioned. The Coke and copy machines were removed, but I was able to keep the refrigerator, which was great for keeping the children's water bottles cold and freezing popsicles for a treat. I worked as hard as I could to get the place in shape, and when my first day of teaching arrived I had transformed the staff room into a real classroom.

You and your students will be spending most of the day in your classroom. It makes sense to make this a comfortable, inviting, and inspiring place to be. The more homey your classroom, the more relaxed your students will feel, and relaxed students take greater risks in learning.

If your classroom looks anything like mine did when I moved in, you have a lot of work to do.

Here are some of the things I've done in my classroom:

# Furniture Arrangement

Start by arranging your furniture. It helps to consider what the traffic patterns might be throughout the room. For example, will the students be able to move easily from the circle area to their desks, or will obstacles be in their way? I found that sketching out the room and furniture placement helped me to decide on my room arrangement. It also saved me the trouble of moving heavy pieces of furniture again and again.

I teach in a small portable classroom. To make more space for my students, I placed most of the bookshelves, worktables, and computer tables along the walls. If space isn't a problem it is useful to partition off parts of the room with the furniture for different areas of study. You can create a circle area this way, or a class library, a computer corner, a writing/reading corner, a science or math corner, or a free-play corner—and don't forget a teacher corner.

I recommend arranging the student desks in small groups. Because of class size reduction in California, I have a maximum number of twenty children in my classroom. I arrange the desks in five groups of four. The desks are pushed together so that the students can face each other when working. This arrangement facilitates working in cooperative groups. They are already face to face for communication and partnered with the student sitting next to them.

Whatever way you choose to arrange your student desks, be sure the children can easily see you while you teach a lesson, and that you can monitor the students in every area of the room, no matter where you are.

## Other Comforting Room Additions

Here are a few more things that will make your room a welcoming learning environment.

*The Primary Teacher's Survival Guide*

## Figure 1–1    Sketch of room arrangement

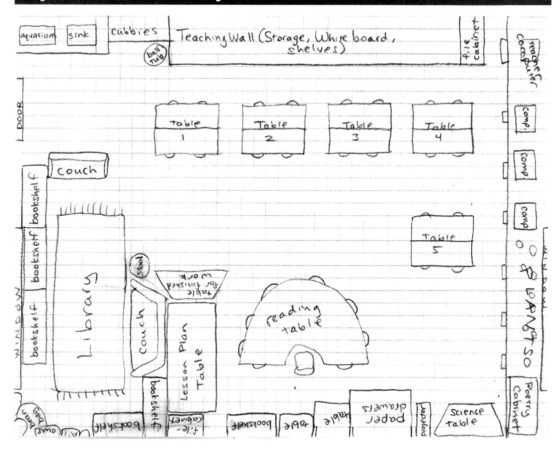

## Plants

Place them on windowsills, bookshelves, and student desks. I've found inexpensive flora at large discount hardware stores for $1 a plant; I've also brought in clippings from plants at home, and from friends and coworkers. They start out small, but it is fun for you and your students to watch them grow. You may even want to measure and chart their growth weekly.

## Floor and Table Lamps

I used my classroom as an opportunity to unload all the old lamps in my apartment, so I could replace them with newer, more stylish ones. This opportunity can be extended to friends and relatives. Inexpensive lamps can also be found at second-hand stores and large discount stores like Wal-Mart.

**Figure 1–2 My classroom**

## Curtains

This is an item I have not acquired yet. I was thinking I'd make my own, or buy the fabric and find out if any of my students' parents were willing to sew them. I've also seen ready-to-hang curtains at home decorating stores. I'm looking for a good sale.

## Homey Furniture

Couches, chairs, and end tables: Here again, I've brought in a couple of pieces from home, but most of the furniture in my classroom I've found at school. We have an area full of unwanted furniture. It was there that I found a child's sized couch. Garage sales are great places to find inexpensive furniture as well.

## Pillows

Place pillows on the furniture and floor. I bought a couple of my pillows on sale at Target, but mostly they came from home.

## Student Work and Paintings on the Walls

You don't need to spend money here unless you want to buy frames. Most student work looks just fine mounted on a piece of construction paper.

*The Primary Teacher's Survival Guide*

### Stuffed Animals

I began teaching with a big brown bear I bought at Target and a few other animals I had been hanging onto from childhood (the ones with no sentimental value). My collection grew quickly. Every Christmas, Valentine's Day, and last day of school my students give me a couple more. I don't ask for stuffed animals, I just get them. You probably will too.

### Area Rugs

Luckily, I had an unused area rug at home. I've seen inexpensive ones on sale by the side of the road here in the city and I've also seen them at discount stores. Be patient and keep your eyes open. Garage sales are a great resource too. You might also want to check with your local carpet store for seconds or large scraps.

### Fresh Cut Flowers

If you are lucky enough to have a yard and garden, bring in your own clippings. I live in an urban apartment. The only time I have flowers is when someone gives them to me. I always have a vase ready.

## Circle Area

A circle area is important, especially for primary grades. It creates a space in which students sit together for lessons, class discussions, and stories. The size of your area depends on how many students you have and how big they are. It should be large enough for all of your children to sit in one large circle comfortably.

I have an inexpensive Persian-type rug in the middle of my circle area. It makes the space seem more like a cozy living room. Put a chair in your circle area so you can comfortably sit. Your students can sit at your feet facing you. I sit on a small couch instead of a chair, with a floor lamp for reading.

## Class Library

Because I have limited space, my circle area is also my classroom library. The bookshelves surround the circle area, creating an intimate space for reading.

During my first year of teaching I had hardly any literature for my students, with the exception of the anthologies from which we were re-

**Figure 1–3   My class library**

quired to teach. I received some donations from teachers who were cleaning out their bookshelves and I bought other books with a minimal amount of supply money. It wasn't much, but it was a start. Student book orders are largely responsible for the considerable number of books I now have in my classroom. Every month I take advantage of low prices and use whatever bonus points I have to get free books. If you don't have many books, don't worry. It won't be long before you accumulate a larger collection. I started with about twenty books, and now, after six years I own over 2000. If you start with very few books, you won't need to refer to the following section on organizing the library until next year, although reading it now may help you to plan ahead.

### Library Organization

The way you organize your library depends on the grade level of your students. No matter how you decide to arrange your library, always model how you expect your students to remove the books from the shelves, read by carefully turning the pages, and put the books back where they belong. A helpful activity to do at the beginning of the year is to remove one book from the library for each child. With the students sitting in front of you in the circle area ask them where each book belongs, then choose a volunteer to put it away while everyone watches. Here are some ideas on organization:

- Very simply, separate the picture books from the chapter books. Remember to teach your students how to tell the difference between the two.
- Categorize the books by subject, theme, and/or author. This is the way I organize my library. For example, I have ocean books, Eric Carle books, and Halloween books in separate tubs (like the kind you use for washing dishes). The books that don't fit into categories go onto a fiction shelf or a nonfiction shelf. I start out the school year with only the fiction and nonfiction books plus books in whatever theme I am using that month. As the school

**Figure 1–4  Theme tubs**

year proceeds I bring out books for new themes. This way, I am always adding new books to the library and student interest is kept high. I teach the difference between fiction and nonfiction books. An easy way for students to remember the difference between the two is fiction = fantasy (both words start with *f* ) and nonfiction = not fantasy. Books that don't fit in either category, such as poetry books, go in a separate tub or area. To practice understanding the difference between fiction and nonfiction, I pull books off the shelves such as I described earlier, and the children decide if they are fiction or nonfiction. They then put the books back where they belong. Every time I read a book I ask, "Is this book fiction or nonfiction?" I put each category of books in a separate tub or basket labeled with its name.

- Simply separate fiction from nonfiction books. You may want to put these books in alphabetical order on the shelves (see following).
- Alphabetical order is the traditional way to organize your books. First, you need to decide if you will alphabetize the first letter of the author's last name or the first letter of the title. In the 2nd and 3rd grade I would choose the title. It is difficult in the beginning for the students to remember the names of authors; they are more likely to remember the name of the book. In 4th and 5th grade I would use the author's last name to teach the traditional method of alphabetizing books.

Children begin to learn ABC order in 2nd grade. I don't recommend alphabetizing your books for kindergarten and 1st grade because at that age many of them are still learning their letters. You can make ABC order easier for your students by color-coding your books. You need as many colors as you can find of masking tape, or plain tape and permanent colored markers. Put a piece of tape on the spine of each book and write on it the first letter of the title (use permanent marker). If you are using colored tape be sure that all the A's are one color, the B's another, etc. You won't be able to find 26 different colors of tape, so you will need to repeat the colors for different letters. If you are using plain tape, make a colored dot with marker for each letter of the alphabet. For example, A, green; B, red; etc. I know you will have a limited number of colors, but having a color and a letter to reference even if the color is repeated for another letter will make putting the book away easier for your students.

### Other Library Ideas

It is fun for the students if you invite one or two children per week or month to pick out their top ten book recommendations. Create a special tub for that student and put the books inside. This can be a special category in your library for students to choose from. To extend the activity ask the child to tell the class why they recommend each book or to write a small book review. This activity can help the child learn how to think and talk about a book. The *Reading Rainbow* video series can help your students get started. Show them the book review section on each tape. Ask them what made each book review interesting and special.  Talk with them about the details used in the review, how the characters were described, what words made them want to read the book themselves, and if the ending was given away. Then ask them to write their own review of a book they love. You may even want to videotape their report like on the *Reading Rainbow* series. These videos are especially fun to watch at open house.

## Learning Centers

A learning center is a special table or area of the classroom where a small group of students can work together on a small project or explore educational materials. Usually learning centers are not used on the first day or even first weeks of school. They take time to organize, set up, and teach. It is better to wait until you know your students and they have become accustomed to your teaching style, classroom, and rules. Because learning centers are a complex, involved teaching technique I am choosing not to explain how to implement them here. To truly do the subject justice I would need to write another book. Your resources for learning centers include coworkers, workshops, and books on the subject found at the teacher supply store.

I recommend the following titles:

*Developing Literacy Using Reading Manipulatives* by Sandi Hill, Creative Teaching Press, 1997
*Instant Math Centers, Hands on Independent Math Activities K–1 and 2–3* by Janet Bruno, Laura Means, Liz Newman, and Glenda Nugent, Creative Teaching Press, 2000
*What Are the Other Kids Doing While You Teach Small Groups?* by Donna Marriott, Creative Teaching Press, 1997

**Figure 1–5    Student book review**

Brianna

Magic tree house #3 Mummies in the morning by Mary Pope Osborne

Hi! My name is Brianna. I chose this book out of the liberary. And once I red it I was amased. I like this book because Jack, and Annie do alot of.... exiting, skary, supper, cool edventures.

If you like chapter books about kids you should get Magic tree house 3 Mummies in the Morning

*The Complete Guide to Classroom Centers*, Creative Teaching Press, 1996.

There are many benefits to using learning centers. Learning centers can encourage student-to-student communication, which is especially helpful to second language learners. They can foster independence and responsibility, give your students a chance to learn and work on their own at their own pace, and allow you time to work with small groups or individual students. Previously taught lessons can be reinforced in centers and opportunities presented to enrich the curriculum and interdisciplinary content.

## Bulletin Boards

I recommend keeping your bulletin boards simple so they are easy to change and update.

An important purpose of bulletin boards is for displaying student work such as writing, art, show-and-tell, and science or social studies reports. If my classroom has sufficient wall space, I create a bulletin board to display student work in each subject. It is important that all students be represented by their work. If only the best work is displayed you will be fostering a competitive environment and lower the self-esteem of students who are below average. A creative writing board, science board, and math board would be the bare minimum. Cover each of your bulletin boards with plain paper and surround it with a border. I recommend using the same color as a backing for each display. When many different colors are used it may make the room look overly cluttered. These bulletin boards can be left up all year. The only thing you need to change is the student work.

Another type of bulletin board can include teaching materials for the curriculum or special skills. For example, because I have many second language learners in my classroom, I like to create a monthly bulletin board with important vocabulary for the theme of the month. In September I focus on fall and back-to-school themes. I tack up leaves of different colors, pictures of trees, rakes, apples, and school supplies, each with the name of the object underneath. Other bulletin boards may display parts of speech, mathematic place value, geometric shapes, the parts of a leaf, or problem-solving skills.

Lastly, bulletin boards can be informative about ongoing events. You may want to have a bulletin board for parents on which you may display

**Figure 1–6    A simple bulletin board**

**Figure 1–7    A theme bulletin board**

current flyers sent home from school, upcoming school events and calendar, a list of supplies that are needed, a list of great websites for kids
and parents (or website of the week), a classroom newsletter, or articles
on how parents can help their children at home. Another bulletin board,
for students, might include information such as the schedule, school cal-

**Figure 1–8   Birthday chart**

**Figure 1–9   Partial alphabet chart**

endar, homework assignments, current lunch menu, and student of the week, in which the student is honored for her uniqueness, upcoming birthdays, school announcements, or photos from the last class party.

## Other Uses of Wall Space

Motivational posters can be used, (celebrating ethnic diversity, community, scientific achievements, nature, and art.)

### Birthday Chart

Display student birth dates by month. Make your own or buy premade charts at your local teacher store.

### Alphabet Chart

An alphabet chart can be found at your local teacher supply store.

### Number Line

There are different kinds of number lines. Some just have numbers, others have pictures and numbers. Again, these can be found at the teacher supply store.

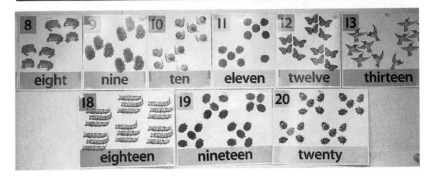

**Figure 1–10  Partial number line**

## Calendar

I use a pocket chart calendar that I change every month, a hundreds chart, money chart, place value chart, number line, weather graph, season chart, paper for writing the current time, and paper for writing daily equations. I highly recommend Box It or Bag It Math (see the Epilogue for my list of recommendations) for ideas on how to use the calendar as a teaching tool.

## Book Covers

Don't know what to do with the book covers that came with your hardbound books? Put them on the walls in your classroom library.

## Student Photos

I also use pictures of my students doing class projects or on field trips and portraits.

## Clothesline

If you are short on wall space in your classroom you might want to try hanging a clothesline from wall to wall. Be sure to check with your custodian first to make sure you are not breaking a fire code. To hang your clothesline, screw a hook or eyelet into opposite walls and high enough so that when you attach the rope and hang student work, you won't get hit in the head. Tie the rope tightly to both sides or the weight of the papers you hang will pull it down. Student work can be attached with clothespins. Because the clothespins are easy to take down and rearrange, you can rotate the work frequently.

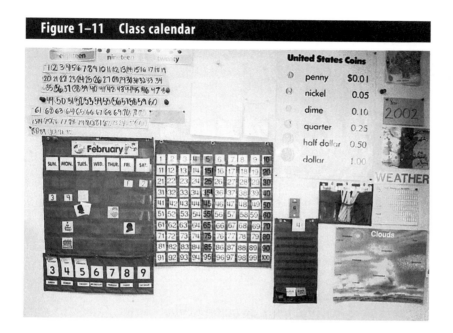

**Figure 1–11   Class calendar**

## *Final Thoughts*

As you can see from reading the ideas I've outlined in this chapter, you have endless options in creating an effective classroom environment. I liken the process to decorating my apartment. Have fun with it. Shop around. Look at what your coworkers have done with their rooms. Take all the best ideas and make them your own.

# *How Do I Survive the First Days of School?*

There were ten minutes to go before school started. I was very nervous. The night before I had lain awake in anticipation of such a pivotal point in my career. I must have gone over the day's plans in my head twenty times. Now, with so little time before my big moment, I walked into the office one more time to check my mailbox. No mail. Back in my classroom I did my tenth walk-through to make sure everything was in place. The bell rang. I greeted my new students at the door with a handshake. Many of them looked more nervous than I. To my surprise, they took their seats in total silence, then looked up at me waiting for class to begin. I nervously began to speak and after just a few moments felt like I had been teaching for years. By 10:00 AM I had finished all the lessons I had planned for the day. Now what was I to do?

Your first day of class may not be far away. This chapter gives you some tools and ideas about how to spend your first few days of teaching.

## *Before the First Day*

Before the first day there are a few things you need to do.

- Get familiar with the school layout. Walk around; find the staff room, library, PE room, lunch area, copy room, supply room, bathrooms, and computer lab.

- Get to know the names of the staff members. Keep a list of the staff on hand, even better, the last staff picture.
- Look through the school calendar and mark important events on your personal school calendar and lesson plan book.
- Get to know the student names. If a name is difficult to pronounce, ask that child's teacher from last year how to pronounce it correctly. Last year's yearbook and school photos can also help you in learning student names.
- Purchase snacks for your class to distribute the first few weeks of school. The children won't be used to going so long without eating and may even complain of hunger within an hour of school starting. I recommend crackers, juice boxes, fruit, popcorn, pretzels, yogurt, fruit rolls, and cheese.
- Overplan. There is nothing worse than running out of things to do on the first day of school. Prepare to teach twice as many lessons as you think you need. Anything you don't have time to teach can be rolled over into the next day.
- Examine cumulative folders. Many teachers like to look through the cumulative folders of their students so that they can learn more about them and be prepared for any challenges they may have. I don't recommend doing this. I prefer to start the year fresh without any preconceived opinions about my students. That first impression you get from their folder may stick with you for the entire school year. For example, if the file says a student has behavior issues, you might start the school year thinking that the child is difficult or a troublemaker. I've discovered that children who had behavior issues the previous year don't necessarily have them when they come to my class. This could be due to a couple of things: The child matured over the summer; last year's teacher's idea of a discipline problem is different from mine; or the child had a personality conflict with the last teacher. Whatever the case, I don't reference the cumulative folder until I feel I need more information.

# The First Day

## Meeting and Greeting Students and Parents
Be friendly and warm when greeting your new students and parents.

They may be nervous about meeting the new teacher and worried that you might not like them. I like to welcome my students by greeting them at the door and asking them their name, shaking their hands, and introducing myself. Even the younger kids love this. I let them find their seat while I greet the parent or the next child. Try to catch the parent's name and commit his face to memory. This helps you to be sure the correct person is picking up the child and know the parent when you meet him again.

Learn student names quickly. It helps to use their names repeatedly throughout the day. Take every child's picture and get it developed immediately. This way you can practice matching their names with their faces. If you are not sure how to pronounce a child's name, ask the child. Names are identities; if you pronounce a child's name wrong, the child may feel you are not seeing the child for who she is.

Don't forget to smile. You may be so worried and serious about things going well that you look unhappy. I was so excited on my first day that my face hurt from smiling too much. Either way it is best to be natural and calm, letting your personality shine through all the hard work it took to get you where you are. Be natural. Be yourself.

Sometimes parents like to come into the classroom to watch class begin, especially in the lower grades. Every teacher is different in how she handles observing parents. Most parents won't stay for more than fifteen minutes. Usually they just want to make sure their child is okay, or get a feel of the classroom atmosphere. On my first day of teaching a couple of parents lingered for more than half an hour. I felt uncomfortable being observed for so long but didn't want to be intrusive by asking them to leave. One parent stayed until recess time. I have since learned that it is okay to ask the parents to leave after school starts. I explain that their child is in good hands, promise to call if there are any problems, and ask if they have any questions. Ask the whole class to wave goodbye and say, "We'll see you after school!"

# Establishing Routines

Starting on the first day you should begin to establish classroom routines. Your students will be learning the procedures that will help keep your classroom a calm and unchaotic place. Model everything. In other words, show your students exactly what you expect them to do by doing it yourself in front of them. For example, don't just tell the class to walk to the circle and sit down. You sit at a student desk, get up, push in the chair, walk to the circle area, and sit down with your legs crossed. I show my students how to put the crayons away neatly, walk to the water fountain, sharpen pencils, and line up. Everything has its place in the classroom. I leave almost nothing for them to question, and in that way they begin to become self-sufficient.

The more your students can do themselves, the more they learn. The less time you spend on details, such as sharpening pencils, the more time and energy you will have to devote to teaching subject matter to your students. The more work you have to do, the more stressed out you will feel. When you cultivate independence in your students, your classroom will run smoother, your students will take pride in what they can do on their own, and you will be free to guide and support student learning, which is what you were hired to do.

## Procedures

Spend at least fifteen minutes every day for the first two weeks of school teaching the classroom procedures and rules. Please see Chapter 3 , How Do I Implement Classroom Management? for more information on rules.

### Sharpening Pencils

Even an action as simple as sharpening a pencil should have a procedure. Otherwise, your students may disrupt the class by sharpening their pencils at an inappropriate time. Here is what I do:

I place a container next to the pencil sharpener for broken or dull pencils. At the end of the day I assign one student the job of sharpening. Or, if there isn't enough time, I sharpen them myself after school.

### Retrieving Supplies

Most of my students' supplies are kept in baskets on their desks and are easy to access. The supplies are anything used on a regular basis. My students always have pencils, erasers, crayons, markers, colored pencils, scissors, and glue. There are occasions when the children need other materials like tissue paper, glitter, or rulers. I make sure they know where to get these supplies ahead of time. I call the students by tables

**Figure 2–1   Supplies on student desks**

to retrieve them. If your students need to get up to get other supplies, model walking to where the supplies are stored, choosing what they need, and returning to their desks. Do the same for returning supplies.

## Getting Attention

Here are some different ways of getting the attention of your students when they are in the middle of an activity. I teach each of these techniques by explaining the procedure first, modeling the behavior myself, asking a student to model, and then practicing over and over again throughout the day. I don't recommend using all of these techniques; too many may confuse the children. Instead, teach one or two and go from there.

### Freeze

Use a signal to stop all motion and noise in the classroom so that you can give further instructions to all students.

### Nonverbal Commands

I ring a bell, tap a triangle, play the piano or other instrument, and, my favorite, play the rainstick, a South American musical instrument that sounds like rain falling, to get the children's attention. The reason

I love the rainstick is because it is a loud but gentle sound that lasts for about fifteen seconds. This gives the students a moment to notice that the class is being asked to freeze. I also love to hear a live instrument. As for most bells, I personally find them irritating.

When the students hear the signal they stop what they are doing, put all their materials down, put their hands on their heads, and look at me. I recently added putting their hands on their heads because my young students were so engaged in their work they didn't want to stop and listen.

Teach your students the peace symbol. When you need their attention, hold your fingers up. When everyone is doing the same (silently of course), you can address them.

Also try snapping and clapping a pattern, letting all the children join in. When everyone is involved, stop and ask for their attention.

## Verbal Commands

* "One, two, three, eyes on me!"
* "If you can hear me, touch your head, if you can hear me, touch your knees, if you can hear me look at the door. . . ." and when you have their attention, "If you can hear me, look at me!"
* Sing a song the entire class knows, for example, "The Itsy, Bitsy, Spider." When the song is over you have their attention.
* Count down from ten, when you get to zero the children freeze. For a variation try counting up to 100 by tens or fives, or counting to twenty by twos.

**Figure 2–2 My rainstick**

### Not Recommended

* Flipping the light switch on and off. This can cause seizures in students with certain medical problems.
* Yelling: This might make them quiet, but can be very upsetting to children. It's disrespectful. How would you like it if teachers yelled at you every time they wanted your attention? Yelling also contradicts itself. Why would you yell if you wanted the outcome to be silence? Your students will have more respect for you if you are calm and composed. If you yell all the time you might find yourself in the principal's office explaining why several parents have complained about your discipline techniques. At the very least, you may earn yourself a reputation as a *mean* teacher.

## Coming in When School Starts

Do you want your students to go to their seats or the circle area when they come in? I recommend they go to their seats on the first day because you can supervise them easier. Also, you have not taught them how you expect them to sit in the circle area. One year I asked my students to wait for me in the circle as I greeted parents at the door. When I turned around my students were rolling on the floor and throwing pillows!

Play soft music in the background as students enter the room. My favorites are *The Four Seasons* by Vivaldi, anything by Carlos Nakai (a Native American flutist), and the local classical radio station. Instrumental music works best. If you chose music with vocals, your students may enter the room singing (which may be what you want) or they may act silly. For example, imagine all your students pretending to sing along with your favorite Barry Manilow song.

Leave a coloring page, journal, or other assignment on their desks that they can begin working on as soon as they sit down.

Keep a basket of books on each table so the students can read quietly at their desks when they enter the classroom.

Remember, how you start the morning will set the tone for the rest of the school day.

When I take attendance every day I say "Good morning" to each child, make eye contact, and smile to acknowledge the child's presence. I make a point of talking to each of my students every day to say something positive, even if it is just for a minute. In doing this I hope to make everyone feel special and important.

## Bathroom Use

Though it is better for children to use the bathroom before school, at recess, lunch, and after school so that they don't miss instructional time, there are always exceptions. Children have the right to go when they need to. It is important to be kind and sensitive when your students ask to use the bathroom. Not letting them go can result in bladder infections. Remember, some of your students may have medical conditions, which cause frequent urination.

Children have also been known to take advantage of the right to use the bathroom. It is important to establish rules and procedures, but you may want to look into why they are asking to leave the classroom so frequently. Sometimes students ask to use the bathroom when the work is too difficult and they need a break, or when it is too easy and they are bored. Here are my bathroom rules:

I only let one boy and one girl go to the bathroom at a time. Through experience I've learned that some children like to leave with their friends, play in the bathroom, and lose a large amount of instructional time. I have one bathroom pass for the girls, and one for the boys. The passes are kept on the door where they are easy to see. If the pass is hanging on the door, the children may ask to use the bathroom; otherwise, it means they need to wait for the last child to return. I ask the children to sign out in a dated page of a spiral notebook. This allows me to keep track of how many times a day the children are leaving the room. If I think there is a problem I can share this notebook with their parents. I also have a special signal the children use when they ask me if they may use the bathroom. I use the okay signal (make a circle with your thumb and pointer finger, the other fingers stand up straight). Any simple hand signal will do. When they use the signal the children can ask to be excused while I'm teaching a lesson. They don't need to interrupt with "Ms. Heyda, may I use the bathroom?"

## Water

I always give the whole class an opportunity to get a drink of water after recess and lunch. I've found it only takes a couple of minutes. The children quietly put their heads down to rest and relax when they come inside. Then I call them by tables to get a drink.

At other times during the school day the general rule is, they may get a drink during seatwork or center work. This helps to avoid the disruption of children getting up in the middle of a lesson.

If your classroom is very hot, I recommend allowing your students to keep water bottles on their desk. This way, they won't need to keep getting up for a drink, and dehydration is prevented.

## Lining Up

To avoid running, pushing, or crowding, I never tell the whole class to line up at one time. Instead I either call the students by their table number, one name at a time, or, I make a game of it. For example, I'd say, "If you are wearing red, line up," or "If your last name starts with letters A–F, line up," or, "If your favorite sea creature is a dolphin, line up."

During the first two weeks of school I ask the class to practice lining up a couple times a day.

Another tool for helping your students line up is to assign each child a number and ask them to stand in numerical order. When in place, you can ask them to count off their numbers. This is an easy way to see if anyone is missing and is especially effective during a fire drill. I also arrange the kids so that they are not standing near other children they are likely to chat or goof around with when they are expected to be quiet.

## Classroom Tour

I like to start the first day of school by taking my students on a classroom tour to help them feel comfortable with their surroundings. They learn where their jackets and coats are hung, and where their lunch boxes, backpacks, and notebooks are kept. Outside my classroom under the window I have a coat rack with a double hook for each child. Unless it is raining, their coats, backpacks, and lunch boxes are hung there. Inside the classroom the students have cubbies for their things. My current room was furnished with built-in cubbies by the door. This is where student notebooks, folders, and binders are kept. I did not have student cubbies or coat hooks when I started my first year of teaching. I solved this problem by asking during back-to-school night if any parents could build me a set of cubbies for the room. One father volunteered. When the cubbies were complete, the children painted them.

The children also learn the different areas of the classroom, where they can find toys for free time, math materials for math time, and where I keep my things. I give them a strong warning that my work area is off limits. My supplies are tucked away in a corner and I try to arrange them so the students are not tempted to play with them. So far I haven't had any trouble with my students touching or taking my belongings. This includes my wallet and purse, which I lock in a file cabinet.

## School Tour

It is also important to take your students on a school tour the first day, preferably before recess. This way your students know where they can find the bathroom, or where to get help if they fall and get hurt. Some of the things you need to show them are the playground boundaries, bathrooms, snack/lunch area, drinking fountains, office, principal's office, bus stop, gym, library, and computer lab. This is a good time to practice walking in a straight line and teach the playground rules. With the permission of your coworkers, walk your students through the other classrooms at the same grade level. As you walk, introduce any teachers and school personnel you meet on the way.

## Student Jobs

You may wish to assign weekly or daily jobs to your students so they can be a part of keeping the classroom neat and running smoothly. I like to assign jobs so I can be fair in letting everyone have a chance to do them. By giving your students jobs you are teaching them to be responsible and allowing them to contribute to the classroom community. Here are some job ideas:

ball monitor (passes out balls)
jump rope monitor (passes out jump ropes)
lights and door monitor (turns out lights and closes the door when the class leaves the room)
hall monitor (ensures safety and order)
chalkboard eraser
recycler (takes out recycling)
line leader
veterinarian (feeds the fish and other animals)
botanist (waters plants)

Figure 2–3    Job wheel

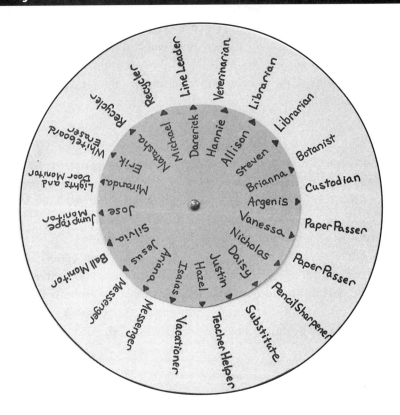

librarian (straightens out library)
custodian (makes sure the top of everyone's desk is clean)
paper passer
pencil sharpener
messenger (takes attendance to the office, etc.)
teacher helper (does special tasks)
substitute
vacationer (has no job for the week)

Teach these jobs by modeling. You may need more than one student to complete some of the tasks. Rotate the jobs so that each student gets to do every job. I have found that the easiest way to do this is by creating a job wheel.

To create a job wheel you need two large pieces of tag board, preferably different colors, a brass paper fastener, and two circular objects that you can trace, one larger than the other, like a garbage can and a large bowl. Trace the circles on the tag board and cut them out. Place the smaller circle on the larger circle and poke a hole through the center of both. Secure the circles with the paper fastener. On the outside circle write the names of each job. On the inside write the names of each child. Do all your writing in pencil first. It can be difficult to line up the names and jobs evenly. Every time you wish to rotate jobs, give the wheel a small turn.

# First-Day Activities

Talk about yourself. Bring in photos and things of importance to you. Show off a special skill or talent you may have. Let your students get to know you. Allow them to ask you questions about yourself. Show your class you're not just a teacher; you're a real person.

The first few days, even weeks, of school are mostly focused on adjusting the children to their new classroom, new teacher, each other, to teaching rules and procedures, schedule, and assessing where the students are academically in different subject areas. Spending a lot of time on these things helps ensure that your future lessons will run smoothly and be geared toward your children's needs. After the adjustment period is over your students will be ready to dive into the rich and engaging curriculum that you provide. Your planning will become easier to do after the schedules for PE, music, and computer lab are set. Use the sample first-day schedule I have written as a guideline.

## Sample First Day

| | |
|---|---|
| 8:30 | Greet students and parents |
| | Review date and schedule |
| | Gather on rug |
| | Take attendance/lunch count |
| 8:45 | Read a story or teach a song |
| 9:00 | Tour classroom |
| | Review school behavior code |
| | Tour school |
| | Pass out snack |
| 10:15 | Recess |

| | |
|---|---|
| 10:35 | Drinks |
| | Review class rules |
| | Play *rule bingo* |
| | Free exploration of math manipulatives |
| | Write about summer vacation |
| 12:00 | Review lunch routine |
| 12:10 | Lunch |
| 1:10 | Drinks |
| | Tour class library |
| | DEAR (drop everything and read) time |
| 1:35 | Start self-portraits |
| | Read a story |
| 2:20 | Clean up/discuss accomplishments/pass out handouts |
| 2:30 | Dismissal |

I don't teach all the rules and routines on the first day. That would be too much, especially for the lower grades. Instead, I introduce new things slowly over the first week.

## General Activities

### Teach a Song

I like to pick a theme song for the class that I teach the first day. My favorite is *Three Little Birds* by Bob Marley. I write the words on a piece of chart paper. Before I teach the song I ask the kids to look at the words and try to read it or find some words that they know. I then read the song as a poem, stopping to explain any words or phrases they might not understand. Then we echo read. I read a line, the students repeat it. Then I sing the song to them, and we echo sing. Finally, I ask for volunteers to make up hand motions to go with each line. For example, in the line "Smile with the rising sun," the students might make a circle with their hands and slowly raise their *sun* while smiling. If the children run out of ideas, I help them. When every line has a motion, we sing the song again with all the motions. We practice singing this song throughout the day. At the end of the week, when the song is memorized, the children take home the song in written form to teach to their parents for homework. This process becomes a routine. I teach a song or poem once a week. When the homework is returned each child puts their song in a personal poetry binder that they can reference throughout the school year and take home in June.

**Figure 2–4 Student self-portrait**

### Read Stories

Find books about the first day of school to read to your students. Also, begin to read stories about whatever theme or subject you will be teaching.

### Write

Ask your students to write about their summer, and what they want to learn in your class. If your students don't know how to write yet, ask them to draw a picture and then dictate to you what they want to say. You write their words below the picture.

### Self-Portrait

Ask your students to draw or paint what they look like. You might want to try yarn for hair and fabric for clothing. The background can be

**Figure 2–5  Guessing game questionnaire**

**Mystery Person**

Favorite animal: _____

Favorite food: _____

Favorite playground game: _____

Favorite color: _____

When I grow up I want to be a : _____

_____

Favorite TV show: _____

_____

I am good at: _____

_____

Hobbies: _____

_____

My Name is _____

their favorite color, place, or something they like to do. This activity works best if you make a sample self-portrait and then model the process. These portraits can be kept on display all year long.

### Guessing Game

The children fill out a questionnaire about themselves. Their age, height, favorite color, birthday, sport, subject, and food. Don't let them sign their names. Read the questionnaire to the class and let them guess the identity of the child.

**Figure 2-6 My favorite math manipulatives**

### Photo with Profile

Take a picture of each of your students. Mount the picture on a nice piece of construction paper. Ask your students to decorate the border.

On a piece of lined paper, ask your students to neatly write their name, age, and some of the things they are interested in or like to do for fun.

Glue both pieces to a large sheet of construction paper to display on the wall. If you can get it done in time, this is a nice display for back-to-school night.

### Math Exploration

Children in every grade level need to get to know their math manipulatives before they use them for problem solving. Math manipulatives are cubes, blocks, bear-shaped counters, plastic chain links, and even dried beans. I recommend Unifix Cubes, Snap Cubes, Pattern Blocks, Color Tiles, and tubs of small plastic animals. I store them on a shelf where the students can easily access them when they need them. Let the children play with and explore the properties of your manipulatives. Otherwise, you might give the students cubes for

*How Do I Survive the First Days of School?* • **31**

**Figure 2–7    How we got to school today graph**

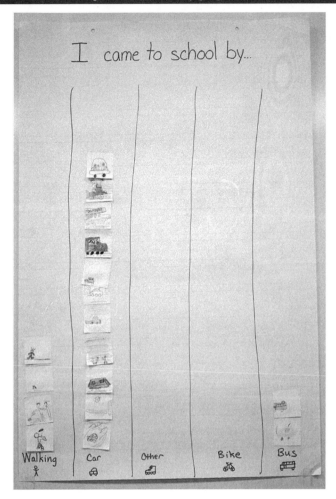

counting and find that everyone is building forts instead of solving math problems. The beginning of the school year is the most appropriate time to do this activity. Put the materials in separate areas and allow your students to play with each. You may want to assign groups or pairs of students to different centers, or let them choose on their own where they want to go. Some materials may be more popular than others, so you will need to limit the number of students in each area.

## Graphs

Creating graphs is a fun way to teach math concepts and for the students to get to know each other. On a piece of chart paper write, "How did you get to school today?" Their choices may be by car, by bus, walking, on a bike, or other. Ask the students to draw a picture of how they get to school on a 2" × 2" piece of paper. When they finish, ask each child to come up to the chart and glue their picture in the appropriate column to create a bar graph. When everyone is finished, ask him or her what he or she notices about the graph. Which way do most kids get to school? Which way do the least number of students get to school? How many more walkers are there than bike riders? Other graphs might show whose class they were in last year, school lunch or home lunch, favorite color, and birthday month.

### Discuss Accomplishments

I like to joke with the children and pretend I'm the parent asking, "What did you do in school today, dear?" Then I'll pretend I'm the child and answer, "Nothing." To change their answer from nothing to something we review the day. I ask the children what they did in school, what they learned, what they liked the best, and what they might try to do better the next day. This helps your students understand how much they have accomplished and gives them something to report to their parents when they go home.

# Final Thoughts

Relax. You've done as much as you can to prepare for your first day. Go home, eat a good dinner, and go to bed early. It may help to set out your clothes the day before and decide in advance what you will eat for breakfast. Talking to a friend can be calming if you're feeling nervous. Write down your feelings in a journal. I recommend getting into the habit of taking a few notes to reflect on student learning, behavior, and the success of lessons every afternoon or evening. If an activity did not work the way you wanted, write down what you would do differently the next time. Everything will be fine.

# 3

# *How Do I Implement Classroom Management?*

Though the days of my job as a substitute teacher are slowly fading from my mind, there are some moments I will never forget. One of these memories was of a 5th grade class. I never knew what to expect when I walked into a classroom to substitute teach. Some days were great; others had me on the verge of tears. With this particular class, I wasn't sure if I wanted to laugh or cry. The class was mostly boys who were difficult to handle. I figured this out not only by the way they acted but by seeing a picture of their teacher, a big husky man who I assumed was a strong disciplinarian. The students had been pushing my buttons all day by shouting out answers, getting up from their seats to sharpen pencils, going to the bathroom without asking, talking when I was teaching, and so on. In the middle of social studies, while they were working in small groups researching the food, clothing, and shelter of the pilgrims, a group of boys went over to the sink for a drink of water. I saw an unusual movement out of the corner of my eye. I turned my head to see bubbles floating through the room. They were blowing bubbles during social studies. "Let me have the bubble container," I demanded. There was none. To my shock and horror, the boys were eating soap and blowing the bubbles out of their mouths! I couldn't believe it. Who ever heard of children voluntarily eating soap? The boys washed out their mouths and went back to their seats. I wrote of the incident in my note to the teacher at the end of the day. I never found out if they were punished.

Good classroom management is vital for good teaching. Chances are if your students are out of control, they are probably not learning as much as they could if the classroom were calm and orderly. It is important to start off the school year by establishing your behavior expectations, rules, and consequences.

Before implementing any classroom rules, check with your principal to learn about any school policies regarding discipline. Also, you may be required to share your classroom management procedures in writing with your principal.

# Who Decides on the Rules?

I prefer to use the school code as my classroom rules. The code is "Be safe, be helpful, be responsible, be respectful, be thankful, and do your best." I start off the school year by discussing what each rule means. Every week after that I take one rule, write it on a piece of chart paper, and ask the kids to brainstorm what the rule means and what it looks like. This helps them feel more a part of the class instead of feeling that the rules have been imposed on them. I guarantee your students will come up with a very long list. We spend about five minutes a day on that one rule, and I write their ideas on the chart. The rules are posted in a central location in the classroom. You can ask the students to sign the charts to make your behavior contract with them more formal.

Remember to explain to your students why each rule is important. For example, I'll tell them that they can't run in the classroom because the space is small and they could trip and fall or run into and hurt one of their classmates. The rules I set are to protect the safety of the students, teach a few basic life skills, and create an environment that fosters learning.

Here are the rules I have in my classroom. They are the specific routines I want the kids to follow in addition to the regular rules. I teach these rules with the rule bingo game described next:

Line up on our class number after recess and lunch.

Keep your hands and feet to yourself.

Keep your table basket neat and clean.

Use the bathroom at recess and lunch, or sign out during class time.

Eat your snack at a table in the snack court.

Recycle all paper.

Raise your hand if you have a question or comment.

**Figure 3–1    Brainstormed rules**

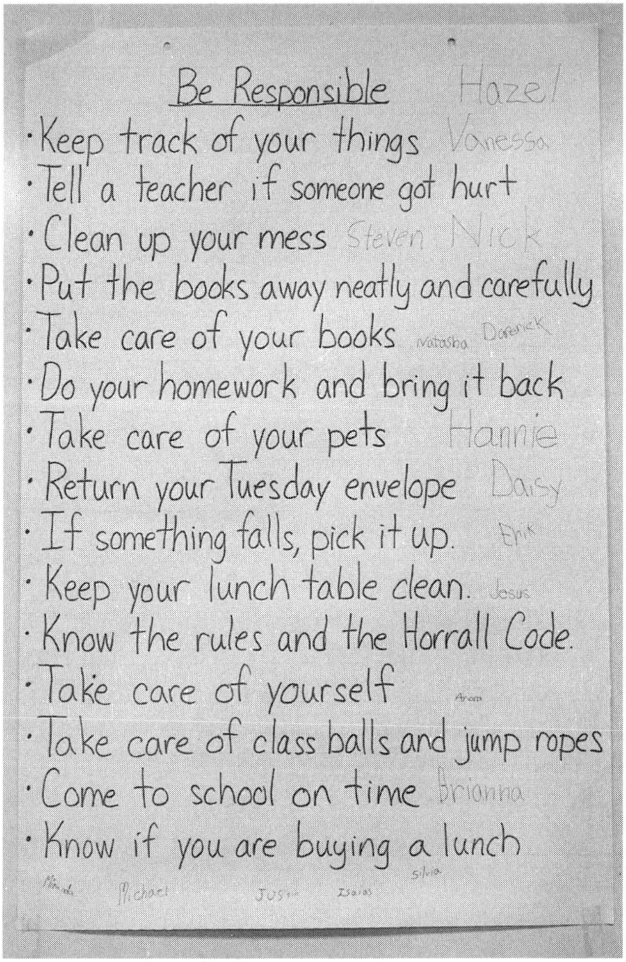

Be Responsible     Hazel
• Keep track of your things   Vanessa
• Tell a teacher if someone got hurt
• Clean up your mess   Steven  Nick
• Put the books away neatly and carefully
• Take care of your books   Natasha  Domenick
• Do your homework and bring it back
• Take care of your pets      Hannie
• Return your Tuesday envelope   Daisy
• If something falls, pick it up.     Erik
• Keep your lunch table clean.   Jesus
• Know the rules and the Horrall Code.
• Take care of yourself     Aaron
• Take care of class balls and jump ropes
• Come to school on time  Brianna
• Know if you are buying a lunch
Nina   Michael      Jose    Isaias      Silvia

Get a drink during seatwork.
Don't run in the classroom or corridors.
Hang up your backpack on the hooks outside the classroom.

# Teaching the Rules

The brainstorming activities I described previously are one technique to teach classroom rules. The following are a few others I have discovered.

**Figure 3–2   Calling card for rule bingo**

Keep your table
basket neat
and clean

### Rule Bingo

This is a game that works best if you create it yourself. You might find rule bingo games at the local teacher supply store that will work for you, but I feel it is more effective when the game is personalized. This game takes time to create. If school is starting in two days I suggest you wait until next year when you have more time to make the game. It is helpful to work with several coworkers who are creating the same rules. That way you can collaborate and share the work involved.

You will need the following items:

a computer program with clip art or your own artistic ability
card stock
bingo chips, or something comparable, like lima beans, to use
as markers

Start by creating the calling cards. Print or draw an icon that represents a rule. For example, for "Use the restroom at recess and lunch," your icon might be the universal sign for men's and women's restrooms. There are many excellent computer programs that will help you easily print out your graphics. Do this for each rule. Make the

*How Do I Implement Classroom Management?*     • **37**

**Figure 3–3    Game board for rule bingo**

cards large enough so that the whole class can see them when you hold them up (about 5½" × 4¼"). To keep your cards fresh year after year, I recommend laminating them.

Next, create game boards (8½" × 11"). Create a grid with nine squares. Inside each square place one of your rule icons or the written rule. Depending on the number of students in your class, create different game boards. It's okay if some are the same, it would be too time consuming to create thirty different boards. The game boards should be laminated as well.

You are now ready to play.

1.  Show your students the icons one at a time and tell them the

rule it represents. I like to have my students repeat the rule after I tell it to them.

2. Give each student a game board and bingo chips. Tell them the goal is to get three icons in a row, horizontally, vertically or diagonally. When they do, they yell, "Bingo!"

3. Hold up the call cards and state the rules. If I have time, I like to play the game until every student wins. I often choose to award them a gummy worm or snack for winning. My students beg me to play the game with them every day. When they know the rules by heart I post the calling cards in a central part of the room for the kids to reference whenever they need a reminder.

## Acting Out Rules (Modeling)

Modeling is another fun way to teach your classroom rules. I start by modeling what a rule looks like. For example, "Throw all paper in the recycling basket." I get up and show what it looks like to put different kinds of paper in the recycling bin. You can do this for all the rules or have the kids model instead.

Put your students in pairs or small groups. Give each group a rule to model. The students discuss the rule and decide on a way to demonstrate it for the class. When all groups are ready, they act out their rule.

The game of charades also works well as a variation on modeling. The whole class gets involved in trying to guess the rule being acted out.

Other games to try might be a class rule crossword puzzle, word search, or hangman to fill in extra time at the end of a lesson.

## Student Posters and Stories

A poster or story assignment is a great way to assess student understanding of the class rules. Assign each student a rule. Ask them to either create a poster showing what that rule means or write a story of why that rule is important. For example, students can explain their own personal story about something that happened when they or someone they know was not following the "Be safe" rule. The posters can be hung in the classroom or hallways. The stories can be hung on the wall or put together in a class book. You might want to assign one student per week to bring the book home to share and discuss its content with their families. To make the book more interactive, it is often helpful to include blank pages at the end of the book for parent comments.

# Consequences

As you probably well know, a set of consequences is needed for breaking class rules. Keep in mind that your punishments should be reasonable. Not too lenient and not too extreme. For instance, you wouldn't send a child to the principal's office for calling out instead of raising his hand. Or, if a child punched a classmate, you wouldn't let her go with just a warning. Here is what I do when a child repeatedly breaks classroom rules:

> The first time a rule is broken: I give a warning.
> The second time: I give five-minute time out at their desk with their head down.
> The third time: I give ten-minute time-out and a phone call home after school.
> The fourth time: I send the child to the principal's office, call home, and possibly send the child to detention.

If the student's offense is severe enough, I'll skip several of these steps. For example, if the child punched a classmate, he might go directly to the principal's office. It's your call. You know your students the best. Just remember to always be respectful of the children while disciplining them. It is the behavior that is unacceptable, not the student.

# Awards

One of the nicest ways to encourage good behavior is through positive reinforcement. There are many ways to show students that they are doing a good job. Verbal praise is the easiest. When you see students doing an excellent job, tell them. Give the child specific feedback so he knows exactly what action, behavior, or work was good and why. Was the child quiet at an assembly? Did the child remember to raise his hand? If you have students who repeatedly have trouble following one or more of the rules, praising the child for when she does behave can encourage more of that good behavior.

Sending a quick note home to the parents saying "Congratulations! Your child had a great day today!" and a sentence or two to explain why can be an effective award as well. This helps with parent/teacher communication, and the parents won't get that sinking feeling of "what has she done now" every time you call or send a note home.

Special privileges can also be appropriate student awards. Some ideas are eating lunch with the teacher, free time, exclusive playtime with the class hamster, computer time, being the teacher's helper for the day, and being allowed to bring in an extra item for show-and-tell.

Lastly, there are awards of candy, food, and toys. I generally don't use these because they are materialistic, and children come to depend on them instead of just feeling proud of themselves for their hard work. Candy, food, and toys can also be costly when used on a regular basis. I prefer to save them for special occasions. Stickers are the exception. They are inexpensive, easy to distribute, and the kids love them. For example, if I want the kids to bring back their field trip forms quickly, I'll offer a special sticker in return.

## Documentation

It can be useful to document student behavior for conferences and report cards. Documentation provides you with reliable data and can show improvement or decline in behavior over time. One way to do this is to keep a loose-leaf notebook with a page tabbed for each student. When the child's behavior is challenging, you can briefly document it on her page. This can be done at the end of the day or during class time so you do not forget.

Another method is a point system. This can easily be recorded in your grade book. At the end of the day give each student points: 5 points = great, 4 points = okay, 3 points = poor, 2 points = needs improvement, 1 point = had a seriously difficult day. At the end of each quarter you can add up the points and average them for a grade.

## Implementing Rules

The following techniques for implementing rules also include some techniques to document behavior.

**Figure 3–4    Page from my behavior journal**

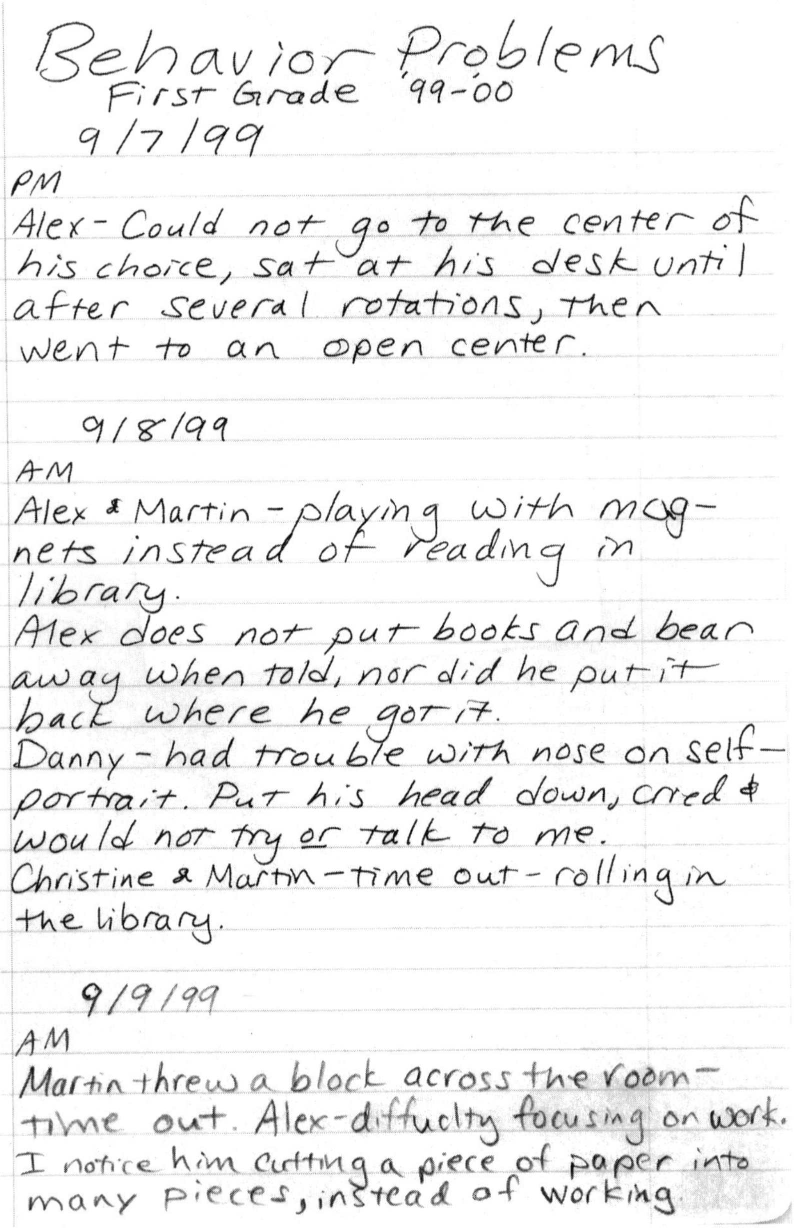

# Behavior Problems
## First Grade '99-00
### 9/7/99

PM

Alex - Could not go to the center of his choice, sat at his desk until after several rotations, then went to an open center.

### 9/8/99

AM

Alex & Martin - playing with magnets instead of reading in library.
Alex does not put books and bear away when told, nor did he put it back where he got it.
Danny - had trouble with nose on self-portrait. Put his head down, cried & would not try or talk to me.
Christine & Martin - time out - rolling in the library.

### 9/9/99

AM

Martin threw a block across the room - time out. Alex - diffuclty focusing on work. I notice him cutting a piece of paper into many pieces, instead of working.

## Figure 3–5   Behavior grade book

First Trimester
PERIOD BEGINNING   8/27
PERIOD ENDING   11/30

SUBJECT   Behavior

CLASS   Homeroom
TIME

| # | Name | 1st Week M T W T | 2nd Week M T W T F | 3rd Week M T W T F | 4th Week | 5th Week |
|---|------|---|---|---|---|---|
| 1 | Alice | 5 5 5 5 | 5 4 5 5 5 5 | | | |
| 2 | Cathy | 5 4 5 5 | 5 3 5 5 4 5 | | | |
| 3 | Daniel | 5 5 5 3 | 5 5 5 5 5 4 | | | |
| 4 | Gabriel | 5 4 5 5 | 5 5 5 5 5 5 | | | |
| 5 | Jake | 5 4 4 4 | 4 5 4 4 5 4 4 | | | |
| 6 | Jim | 4 5 5 3 | 5 5 4 5 5 4 5 | | | |
| 7 | Kimberly | 5 5 5 5 | 5 5 5 5 5 5 5 | | | |
| 8 | Louise | 5 5 5 4 | 5 5 3 4 5 5 5 | | | |
| 9 | Luz | 5 5 5 5 | 5 5 5 5 5 5 5 | | | |
| 10 | Niels | 4 4 5 4 | 5 5 5 5 4 4 5 | | | |
| 11 | Mannie | 4 3 3 4 | 3 2 1 2 3 3 2 | | | |
| 12 | Mary | 5 5 5 5 | 5 5 5 4 5 5 5 | | | |
| 13 | Patty | 5 5 5 5 | 5 3 5 5 5 5 5 | | | |
| 14 | Ramon | 5 4 4 5 | 4 5 5 5 5 5 5 | | | |
| 15 | Raphael | 5 5 5 5 | 5 5 5 5 5 5 5 | | | |
| 16 | Sam | 5 4 5 3 | 5 2 5 4 5 1 5 | | | |
| 17 | Solvig | 4 3 3 2 | 3 3 2 1 2 3 4 | | | |
| 18 | Tammy | 5 3 4 5 | 5 5 5 4 5 5 5 | | | |
| 19 | Ted | 3 4 5 4 | 4 3 3 2 4 5 5 | | | |
| 20 | William | 5 5 5 5 | 5 5 5 5 5 5 5 | | | |

5 = great
4 = okay
3 = poor
2 = needs improvement
1 = seriously difficult day

## Flip a Card

This is my favorite tool for implementing classroom rules. I start by assigning each student a number (this helps protect them from embarrassment). I write each of their numbers on individual pockets in a pocket chart. You can also create your own pocket chart by gluing library envelopes to a piece of poster board. In each pocket are five different colored cards of construction paper. Each color represents behavior for the day. Blue = great, green = okay (student is given a warning), yellow = time-out, red = time-out and phone call home, and white = visit the principal's office, phone call home, detention, or all three.

Every day all children start out on blue. When a student breaks a rule I ask him to go to his number and flip a card. If a child does something severe in nature I might ask her to flip more than one card. At the end of the day I record what color each student is on in my grade

Figure 3–6  Flip a card pocket chart

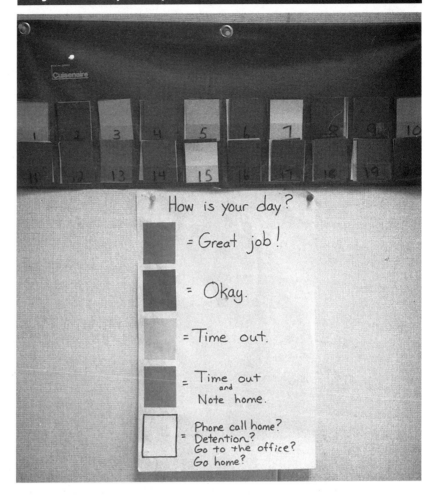

book. I do this by coloring in the square next to the name with a marker (similar to the point system). If a child has been on blue (great) all week long, I send home an award. At conference time I share this chart with the parents and use it in grading on report cards.

## Table Points

Giving table points is a simple technique for when the students are working in groups. Start by assigning each table of students a number, color, or name. You can even let them choose their own. Find a space on the board that is always available and write down their table names. When the tables are working together cooperatively, or si-

**Figure 3–7   Table points**

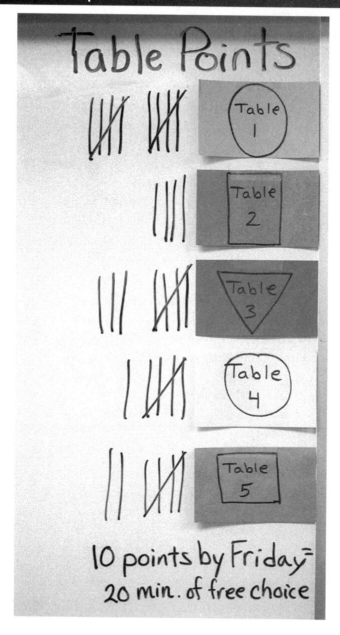

lently, or however you want them to be, give their table a point. I record the points like tally marks because it helps to teach the kids how to count. I set a point goal for the week with an award for meeting that goal. Usually my goal is ten points = twenty minutes of free choice time on Friday when they get to play, draw, read, play on the computer, or just sit and chat.

### Marble Jar

The marble jar is for monitoring and rewarding the behavior of the entire class. When the class is reading quietly or working cooperatively, marbles are added to the class jar. You can help them keep track of the number of marbles in the jar by writing the number on the white board. When the class reaches its goal, let's say 100 marbles, they get some sort of award. This could be anything from free time to a popcorn party.

### Money

This is an excellent tool to use with 2nd grade and up. All students need a coin purse (paper envelope) or a pencil case with their names on it. Positive behavior is rewarded with paper or plastic coins. Realistic paper coins can be found in the back of some math workbooks, or you can buy rubber stamps and cut out the papers you stamped, or just give each student a piece of paper that you stamp when his behavior is good. Your students will be inspired to learn to count money to see how much they have. Set goals such as $1.00 = free time, $2.00 = bring in show-and-tell, $3.00 = lunch with the teacher, $4.00 = a free ice cream. It's up to you. They can keep track of their money in the long-term, or you can wipe the slate clean whenever they meet a goal.

# Consistency

First, be a role model. Be ultraconscious of following all the rules you expect your students to follow. In order for any form of behavior management to work, you need to be consistent in upholding the rules you set. For example, the rule is that students have to raise their hands when they have a question or comment. If a student forgets to raise her hand you might ask her to hold her answer until she remembers the rule. Then another student shouts out an answer and you listen and tell him that was a good job. That inconsistency is showing them that despite the rule about raising your hand sometimes it is okay not to follow it. Even worse, the same student consistently forgets to raise his hand and you honor what he has to say. This teaches the other students that this particular child has the privilege of not having to raise his hand and you are seen as an unfair teacher. No matter how cute or sad my students look, I tell them that a rule is a rule and the consequences are the same for everyone.

Consistency is difficult, especially in the beginning when you have so much on your mind that you don't feel like bothering to enforce the rules every time they are broken. Keep at it. Though it may be hard at first, over time your students will learn what you expect of them and will not need so many reminders on how to behave.

## Community

Community is just as much a part of behavior management as rules and discipline. If students understand and practice respect, responsibility, caring, and cooperation and learn to appreciate their differences they will have created their own community or family in which they are safe to learn, grow, and discover who they are. When community is strong in a classroom, discipline is often unnecessary.

## Handling Difficult Students

### The Conference

Whenever a student is not responding to your behavior management strategies and is becoming a challenge, call in the parents for a parent/teacher/student conference. It is important to have the child there because often witnessing the parent/teacher communication can make her aware of the seriousness of her behavior. Always start your conference by saying something positive about the child (you may have to stretch a little, but be as sincere as possible). Invite the parents to talk about their child. Ask about their home life. There may be a reason for the child's disruptive behavior, such as divorce, family illness, or financial problems. Then explain why you have asked the parents to come in and talk with you. You may want to let the student explain to his parents why you called them in for the conference. This can open up an opportunity for parent/child dialogue. Describe their child's behavior and why it is disruptive. Have your documentation ready to show a record of the child's performance day after day.

Sometimes this conference is all it takes to turn a child's behavior around. Most parents choose to talk with their son or daughter when they get home and will take away a privilege in punishment, such as no TV for a week. Try asking the child how he thinks the problem should be handled. Your conference may open up communication with the parents so that you feel free to contact them when necessary.

## The Behavior Contract

A behavior contract is something that you might want to implement the first time you have a parent/teacher/student conference. Or, you may want to wait and see if the first conference made a difference in your student's behavior.

When you create a contract it is important to involve the child and parents.

First, outline one to three behaviors you would like the child to change. Don't start with more than three or you may overwhelm the child and make the task of improvement too difficult.

Set a goal for what you would like to see the child accomplish in a reasonable period of time. For example, the student will have no more than two conflicts per week with classmates by the end of the grading period. Or, by January the student will be able to focus his attention on his work for ten minutes at a time. Be sure to make this goal very clear for both the student and parents.

Set teacher modifications for the student. What will you as a teacher do to help this child reach the goal? For example, you may choose to create a weekly behavior chart for the student's desk. For each subject or part of the day the child earns a star for good behavior. By having the chart on the desks the student can monitor her own behavior. Your goal may include earning a minimum of three stars a day or having two perfect days per week. If the goal is reached by the end of the week she receives an award. This could be a new sticker for

Figure 3–8   Sample behavior contract

# Behavior Contract

Student Name: _____   Teacher: _____

Parents: _____   Conference Date: _____

## Responsibilities

### Student

Paul will show respect for his classmates by not teasing and calling his classmates names, using swear words in school, and disturbing his classmates during quiet work times. He will monitor his behavior by keeping his behavior chart on his desk. Paul will take his behavior chart home daily to be signed by his parents and return it to school the next day.

### Teacher

Ms. Heyda will monitor Paul's behavior each period. She will award him a sticker on his behavior chart when he has fulfilled the above-mentioned responsibilities. If Paul meets his goals 4 out of 5 times a week, Ms. Heyda will award him with a free ice cream coupon. She will contact Paul's parents immediately upon the event of a severe behavior outburst.

### Parent

Paul's parents will check and sign his behavior chart each day. If his goal has been reached he will be rewarded with a treat or priviledge.

## Goals to be met by April 2002:

Paul will receive a minimum of 8 out of 10 stickers a day for fulfilling his responsibilities of being respectful of his peers.

_____   _____
Student Signature           Date

_____   _____
Teacher Signature           Date

_____   _____
Parent Signature            Date

her folder, a school privilege, or a small eraser. It's up to you and what inspires your student. You may want to send this chart home daily or weekly for the parents to see, sign, and return. The key to making the contract work is creating goals that are realistic for the child. At first the goals might even be easy. As time goes on and the goal is reached, make the task slightly more difficult. For example, change the goal from three stars a day to four.

Set parent modifications for home. What will the parents do differently to help their child reach a goal? This could be agreeing to nightly or weekly discussions about behavior or enforcing the same behaviors at home. The parents can also reinforce good performance in school by awarding and praising their child when she meets a weekly goal. They might choose to take the child out for ice cream, let a friend sleep over, buy a toy, or anything within reason that the child would really like to do or have.

Communication is another key. Your consistent and open communication between child, teacher, parent, and even babysitter, can help keep the child on track at all times. You may keep in touch by phone, e-mail, or letters. Decide if you will talk to them at home or at work. If both parents are working two jobs they may want you to contact them there or send a note home. When both parents speak a language other than English, a translator might be necessary to make the calls for you or to translate your progress reports.

It is important to write the goals and interventions in a contract for student, parent, and teacher to sign. Give a copy to the parent and principal, and keep one for yourself. Please see the attached sample document to use as a guide.

## When Do You Need Help?

Basically, you need help when you have exhausted your resources. You've tried everything you know, from techniques in this book to classroom modifications (moving the child's seat, etc.). You've had conferences with the parents, asked coworkers for assistance, and consulted the child's previous teachers. If you are still struggling with the student after all this, definitely go to your administrator for assistance. You might want to refer your student to a child study team. If you do, be sure to document everything you have done to help your student. Some things I have documented are meetings and phone conversations with the parent, moving the child's seat, time-outs, behavior contracts, and sending the child to the principal's office. You may want to seek help from your administrator before you have exhausted your resources. That's okay too.

# *Final Thoughts*

Sometimes you know the problem is just too big for you to handle. Your classroom isn't an island. When you need it, there is a support network of colleagues, administrators, and organizations there to help you. Reach out, you're not alone.

# *What Are Some Teaching Strategies and Activities I Can Use?*

I was introducing the mathematical concept of sorting by attributes. The week before I had pulled together collections of things to sort like seashells, keys, bottle caps, different kinds of uncooked pasta, and tiny plastic animals. I asked the children to work with their table partners to sort a collection and then raise their hands when they had succeeded. The table with the seashell collection raised their hands first. "How did you sort your seashells?" I asked. One child answered for the whole group: "Johnny thinks his are the prettiest, Jennifer thinks hers are the prettiest, Lisa thinks hers are the prettiest, and I think mine are the prettiest," he replied. The students were carefully guarding their piles of shells. So much for attributes and working together cooperatively, I thought. The answer was the same at each table. Some children literally got into fights over the collections. No one got the concept. I ended the activity feeling very frustrated.

Luckily, that is not the end of the story. I went to my coworkers for help. I learned I left out several important steps like modeling how to work in a group, establishing rules when working in groups, teaching what an attribute is, and modeling and practicing sorting with the entire class. Later I went back to the activity, making sure I covered all the points I missed, and the children sorted like experts.

# Core Curriculum

Before you begin teaching you need to find out what mandatory programs your school district has adopted. Check with coworkers to be sure you have all the teacher-relevant manuals, workbooks, and materials. It is especially helpful during your first year of teaching to have such programs available. They include reading, literature, writing, math, social studies, science, and perhaps English as a second language.

# Thematic Curriculum

In a thematic curriculum all the subjects are woven together. Using a common theme, math is connected to language arts, science to music, and so on. Nothing is taught in isolation. Just like the world we live in, everything is interrelated. Most district-adopted curricula are not thematic. So you will need to design your own themes in the framework of what you are required to teach.

The following example is from an ocean theme I used in my classroom.

### Reading

ocean books, both fiction and nonfiction
poetry about the ocean
myths and folk tales about the ocean

### Writing

fiction: If I were a fish I would . . .
report on your favorite tide pool animal
write your own ocean myth, folk tale, or poem
writing in response to what they learned

### Science

hands-on ocean center with shells, sand, etc.
study how fish breathe underwater

migratory patterns of whales

the water cycle

balanced ecosystems (sandy shore, tide pools, coral reef, deep sea) and how they differ

saltwater plants and animals compared with fresh-water plants and animals

causes of waves and tides

shell identification

### Field Trips

beach or tide pools

aquarium

marine mammal rescue center

zoo

### Music

ocean songs

whale songs

classical music inspired by the ocean

### Art

study paintings of the sea

draw your favorite sea creature

create a classroom kelp forest

### Drama

act out a story like *The Rainbow Fish*

### Dance

dance to the sounds of the sea or imitate sea creatures

### PE

do *The Swim*

swimming lessons

walk like a crab, snail, or seagull

*The Primary Teacher's Survival Guide*

**Figure 4–1    Ocean center**

### Social Action

what we do to save the ocean from pollution
write letters to members of Congress
participate in a beach clean-up day

### Math

What percent of the world is covered with water?
How long is a blue whale (measure with chalk on the playground)?
How much do shells weigh?
How deep does the ocean get?

### Social Studies

early exploration by ship
world trade by sea
how ancient cultures depended on the ocean for survival
the cultures of near ocean and island dwellers
how people depend on the ocean now

### Technology

how people go deep down into the ocean
how people take pictures of the ocean floor

### Recreation

how people travel and enjoy the ocean from kayaks to ocean liners

### Food

seaweed taste test

## Ocean Books

Ocean books I recommend (for teachers):

*Sea Searchers Handbook, Activities from the Monterey Bay Aquarium* by Pat Armstrong, Judith Connor, Chris Parsons, Judy Rand, and Jenny Vuturo-Brady, Roberts Rinehart Publishers, 1996

*The Sea and Other Water* by Marlene and Robert McCracken,
Peguis Publishers Limited, 1985

Ocean books I recommend (for students):

*Is This a House for a Hermit Crab?* by Megan McDonald
*The Whales* by Cynthia Rylant
*The Rainbow Fish* by Marcus Pfister
*Spiny Sea Stars* by Christina Zuchora
Eyewitness Books: *Ocean* by Dr. Miranda Macquitty, *Shell* by Alex
Arthur, *Seashore* by Steve Parker, *Whale* by Vassili Papastavrou,
and *Shark* by Miranda Macquitty
*Gentle Giant Octopus* by Karen Wallace
*My Visit to the Aquarium* by Aliki

### Ocean Videos

*Tales From the Wild, Cara the Sea Turtle* by National Geographic
*Amazing Planet, Creatures of the Deep* by National Geographic
Kids Video

These are just a few examples of the many ways to teach all subjects using one theme.

### How to Pick a Theme

There are many ways to pick themes. Places to look for ideas may be:

- something your students are interested in
- something you are interested in or know a lot about
- a science unit you are required to teach
- a unit in the adopted literature anthology
- a current event topic
- a theme in social studies

### How to Develop a Plan

Start by brainstorming an activity for each subject related to the
theme. Look for teaching books on the subject. For example, the
teacher store has many books on teaching an ocean curriculum.
Check out children's books on the subject. Create some sort of hands-

on center for the students to visit. Look into a field trip that relates to the theme.

# Teacher Strategies

Following are a few strategies you might like to try. They can be used in a wide variety of lessons.

## Setting Goals

Before you teach a lesson ask yourself, "What is the goal of this lesson or activity?" What do you want your students to learn? What skills do you want them to acquire? And do the skills you are teaching reflect the state standards? How does what you are teaching connect to the real world? After all, the school year goes by fast. Don't waste time with lessons that have no value.

## Before You Begin a Lesson

In preparation, reflect on what your students have already learned, or what they might know before entering the classroom. How much of an introduction do you need? Do you need to review a skill previously learned?

## KWL Chart

KWL stands for what we Know, Want to know, and Learned. It helps to connect student learning to what they already know. For this activity create three columns on a large piece of butcher paper. At the top of each write the three topics. Ask the students to tell you things they already know about the subject for the first column. For the second column ask what they want to know. Keep this chart up in a central area of the room. When the lesson or unit is complete, ask the students what they learned and fill in the last section of the chart.

**Figure 4–2   KWL chart**

# The Ocean

| What We Know | What We Want to Know | What We Learned |
|---|---|---|
| Fish live in the ocean. An octopus has eight arms. | How do fish breathe under water. | Fish have gills. |
| Boats sail on the water. | What is the biggest fish in the ocean? | Dolphins are mammals. |
| Some sharks have sharp teeth. | How does the octopus escape danger? | Sharks are fish. |
| | How does the starfish eat? | The whale shark is the largest fish |
| | | Starfish digest their food outside of their bodies. |
| | | An octopus can change its color. |

## Making the Lesson Engaging

The following strategies will help you make your lesson engaging for your students. Whenever possible, avoid a lengthy lecture. Your students will not have sufficient attention span to listen very long. Better results come from dynamic and active lessons.

## Teaching and Presenting

Think about where you are going to teach your lesson. Would it be more appropriate to sit in the circle area? Should the students be in a circle? Will you need to write on the chalkboard? Will the students need to take notes? Will you use the overhead projector or charts that everyone needs to see at one time? Will the students and I have easy access to any supplies we need? Should you stand in one place, several places, or move about the room? As you find your style ask yourself, "Am I moving around the room too much, or not enough? Am I making eye contact with the students? Is my vocabulary understandable?"

## Modeling

Always model every new activity or skill you are teaching before you expect your students to do the task. Watching the flow of the assignment from beginning to end will make it clearer for the children. During my first year I had no samples of what completed work should look like so I completed the assignment myself as a part of the lesson.

I even model my thinking. For example, when solving a math problem I say what I'm thinking out loud to show the reasoning and strategy I used such as counting on my fingers or estimating. Or, I may model how I think of a topic for a story or the best word to use in a sentence. This type of modeling involves metacognition, thinking about thinking. Children using metacognition become aware of their thoughts and develop more ability in thinking through problems.

Here is an example of think aloud language showing the thought process for picking a non-fiction story topic:

"I need to think up a story idea, but I don't know where to start. Hmmm. I'll just look around the classroom and maybe something will give me an idea. I see pencils, but that doesn't remind me of anything. I see the computer, but I don't like computers. I see some balls in the tub. That reminds me I want to play soccer with Karen at recess time. We love to play soccer together, we even play every day after school in my backyard. Hey, maybe I could write about soccer, what I know about soccer, why I like it, who I play with, and maybe I could even tell about the time Karen's dad joined the game and how in the spring I'm going to join the girl's soccer league. Last year I was on the Robins, we came in 2nd place. Yeah, that's a good idea, it's something I love and know a lot about. I'm ready to start writing!"

## Brainstorming

Brainstorming can be used with the whole class or just one person. I brainstormed before I started writing this book. I made a list of all the things I thought a new teacher would need to know, and then later structured these ideas into chapters. Brainstorming allows the children to develop their own ideas. You can ask them to think of story ideas, what they know about plants, winter words, or how to be respectful. When the students come up with their ideas you can write them on a chart as a list, ask the students to take notes, or just keep the activity verbal. Depending on the activity, you may or may not want the children referring to a chart or copying what you've written.

**Figure 4–3    Brainstorming example**

# Writing Ideas

Loosing a tooth
Pets
My last birthday
My favorite holiday
Family vacation
Playground games
Favorite animals
Field trips
When I grow up...
A silly/scary dream

## Visuals

Visual aids are helpful for all students but especially second language learners. Basically anything your students can look at to better understand what you are teaching is a visual aid. Posters, charts, drawings of vocabulary, videos, displays, objects, and modeling are just a few. Be conscious of always having a visual aid to go with what you are teaching.

## Hands-on Experience

Hands-on experience is a powerful teaching tool. There are many different ways to use this technique. You can give your students manipulatives to solve math problems, props to tell a story, or materials to solve a science investigation, anything they can touch, hold, or manipulate. These are often the most memorable experiences your students will have. When I teach the parts of a starfish, I let my students touch and hold a dried starfish. It's even better to hold the live animal at a tide pool or an aquarium; it makes the experience real for them. I am always amazed at how much they remember and learn when they are physically involved in learning.

# Heterogeneous and Homogeneous Grouping

*Heterogeneous grouping* refers to combining students into groups or pairs of mixed ability levels, personality types, or race. This can be advantageous when you want the children to be exposed to different ways of thinking, approaching a problem, and using different work styles.

*Homogeneous grouping* refers to combining students into groups with the same ability level in one or more areas. I do not recommend combining children by personality type, language, or race. This kind of arrangement is racist and prejudiced. Homogeneous grouping is a useful teaching tool when you have several students who need to learn a particular skill. With such a group you can pull them off to the side and focus on the one or many needs they have while the rest of the class does something else. This can be very helpful when teaching reading. Just be careful to keep the groups flexible. Students should be able to move in and out of groups as they improve. Otherwise you are tracking the children and not allowing them to grow to their full potential.

## Students Teaching Students and Communication

One of the most valuable resources you have is your students: students teaching each other and learning together through communication. This works in small groups and pairs. Try them all and choose the ones that best suit the activity or subject. This type of learning can take on many different forms.

### Pairs

A pair of students works together to reach the same goal. For example, solving a math equation, writing a story, or answering research questions. You can let the children decide how they are going to divide the work or give them specific assignments or jobs.

I usually choose the partners I want my students to work with. Ability level and personality are the two strongest factors.

An example of ability level is a child who is very strong in math would not be paired with a student who is very poor in math. The stronger child would be put in a position of being the teacher, and though this is acceptable for certain activities, it takes away from challenging the student in new ways. The student who is poor in math may feel insecure working with such a strong student or may feel overwhelmed and sit back and let the stronger student do all the work. I prefer to pick a partner who is a little above or a little below in ability. This way the children are more likely to challenge each other and feel confident about what they know and can do. The children keep the same partner anywhere from a few weeks to two months, depending on what they are working on and how much improvement I see. For a break in routine, I occasionally let the students choose their own partners. This is usually for a project or activity that is more open ended and less academic.

For personality types, when one child is very extroverted or controlling, I would not pair that child with a child who is very shy and submissive. The extroverted child may take over the whole project or activity and intimidate the shy quiet child. Of course, there are all kinds of exceptions. If the two children described previously were good friends, and very comfortable with each other, the pair might work well together. As with the academic pair, I prefer to pick a partner a little more domineering or less domineering than the other child so they share the work equally.

In the beginning of the school year I prefer to pair girls with girls and boys with boys. I want the children to feel as comfortable as possible, and they tend to feel more at ease if paired with the same sex. By mid to late October I begin to pair boys and girls who feel confident and comfortable with each other. By November I want to be able to pair any child with their best match academically and by personality, boy or girl.

## Cooperative Groups

Small groups of children can work together. Especially with a larger group you will want to model what it looks like when four to five children collaborate. Without modeling, practice, or clear instruction, more outgoing students, or the ones with the most academic strength may take over and complete the work for everyone. In a group of four, one child may be in charge of making sure everyone has an equal turn to talk, another may record the discussion by note taking, one child might be in charge of retrieving supplies, and the last child returns those supplies.

I establish groups in the same way I pair children, using ability and personality factors. This is much more difficult, depending on the size of the group. Tell your students that their groups are subject to change according to how well they work together. If you see that someone is having difficulty, first, try to work out the problem in the present placement. If you see little or no improvement, feel free to place the child in another group. I recommend you make this change the next time the children work in their groups. It could be embarrassing and humiliating to move a child in front of his friends. Before you switch the child, privately let the child know ahead of time that you feel he may be more comfortable in a different group and you'd like him to give it a try.

## The Jigsaw

The jigsaw is an excellent way to teach a large or difficult subject and give students the opportunity for academic collaboration and intellectual discussion and the chance to teach what they learned. In the jigsaw, students are placed in small groups, for example, a group of four. Each child in the group gets a number, one through four. The core group is broken up. All the ones in the class get together, the twos, and so on. In this group they discuss a topic, read a passage, or do some sort of activity. Each number group has a different topic or part of a topic. When the discussion is finished, the children go back to their original groups and report back what they learned or teach the activity.

## The Tea Party

The tea party is another activity that facilitates student/student communication. Line the children up in two even-numbered rows so they face each other. Ask them to take turns explaining to the person across from them the answer to a question you have been studying. For example, "Explain to your partner what things a plant needs to grow." When they are finished explaining, ask one row to move down one person. Whoever was in the front of the line now goes to the back. Then ask another question and repeat the process.

## Music

Music can be incorporated into almost any activity. The easiest way to use music is to play it in the background while the students are work-

*The Primary Teacher's Survival Guide*

ing. Obviously don't play rap or disco, which can be distracting. Stick to new age or classical music, which may relax your students.

It seems a song has been written for just about everything you can think of to teach. In the teacher store I've seen multiplication songs, brush-your-teeth songs, songs about hibernation, and on and on. Before you buy any of these, talk to your coworkers. Teachers who have been in the business for a while may let you borrow what you need. You don't need to be particularly musical or have a great voice to teach a song. My students never seem to notice that I sing out of key.

***Relaxing background music:***

*Mythic Dreamer* by R. Carlos Nakai
*Ancestral Voices* by R. Carlos Nakai and William Eaton
*The Four Seasons* by Vivaldi
*December* by George Winston

***CDs with songs to teach:***

*World Playground, A Musical Adventure for Kids* by various artists
on Putumayo World Music
*We All Live Together, Volume 3* by Greg and Steve
Anything by Raffi

Before you teach a song it helps to know it as well as possible. Memorize the words and tune ahead of time and it will be easier to teach. Write the words to the song on a large sheet of chart paper. I like to give the children an opportunity to read the words to themselves first. If they are not reading yet, I ask them to look for words they know. Then I read the song to them, like a poem. We discuss its meaning and any difficult words. Then I teach the song without the music, line by line. I like to make up hand and body motions to go with the words. This especially helps those students just learning English. It is fun to ask the students to invent motions too. They are often more creative than I and are more likely to remember what they invent themselves. When all the motions and words are learned I add the music.

## Games

Games are another engaging teaching tool. Don't forget to make learning fun. From alphabet bingo to Go Fish, from matching vocabulary with pictures to computer games, your students will get excited about what they are learning. Invent your own activities, ask colleagues for ideas, or look through the thousands of teaching books available. Also, refer to the list of center books in Chapter 1 for books with educational games you can make yourself.

### For Reading

alphabet bingo
beginning and ending sounds bingo
rhyming bingo

### For Math

Go Fish

### For Rainy Days

Candyland
Chutes and Ladders
Dominos
Twister
all kinds of puzzles

### For the Computer

Kid Pix
Sammy's Science House
Baily's Book House
Thinking Things
Reader Rabbit
Kid Works 2
Stickybear Reading
Logical Journey of the Zoombinis

## Drama

I love using drama in the classroom and so do the children. Usually I use it with the literature I am required to teach. After reading a story the students help me compile a list of characters and props. We gather the materials and act it out. At times the children read the dialogue out of their books, at other times I cue them and they ad lib. Either way they get to know the story well. I keep it simple. No fancy sets or backdrops. We mostly use our imagination.

Small groups of children can also act out stories they've written themselves. Even something so simple as "I like rainbows and flowers" can be acted out with hand motions. Try it. Your students will want to write and act all day long.

Another idea is a puppet show. Let your students work in a small group to draw all the characters in their favorite story. The drawings can be glued to craft sticks to make puppets. Background scenery can be drawn on a piece of paper and taped to a chair or wall. Your students will have fun acting out the story and may even want to perform for the class.

## Video

Our county has an extensive library of educational videos. I like to order anything connected with the subject I am teaching. Always remember to preview your videos before showing them. One time I did not preview a video about seeds and plants, assuming there would be no questionable content. Wrong! I think I was more embarrassed than the kids when the narrator explained about the "male and female sexual organs" of plants.

Make your students accountable for what they are learning. If you are showing a video for educational purposes, you don't want your students spacing out during the film. Here are some ideas to make good use of this technology:

- Use the pause button. Stop the tape and explain complicated terms, or ask the kids to retell what they just learned.
- Ask the students to either remember or write down two things they learned from the video. Afterward have them walk around the room and share those two things with five people. Or afterward, brainstorm everything they learned on a piece of chart paper. You can also ask them to write a paragraph about what they learned, or the old standbys, take notes or give a quiz.

## Class Discussions or Debates

Create a mildly controversial situation and have them try to take sides. The students may even need to research the issue to make a strong argument for or against it.

## Worksheets

Worksheets can be useful at times but not as a primary teaching tool. Always remember to model what you expect your students to do. I like to put my children in pairs or groups, unless of course I am assessing what they know.

## Field Trips

Some of the most powerful learning experiences my students have had are on field trips. It is important to prepare your students ahead of time by teaching at least some of the unit or curriculum before you go. It helps when the kids have background knowledge they can apply to what they see and do. For example, my students learned all about tide pool animals before we went to the tide pools. When they got there they were able to identify almost everything they found. It was very exciting. When you return, have a follow-up activity planned either for that day or the next. Asking the students to write about what they learned and experienced is an easy way to bring closure to the trip.

### Setting up a Field Trip

Some of the things you need to consider when taking your class on a field trip are presented here.

#### At Least a Month before the Trip

- Reserve admission ahead of time.
- Transportation: If taking the bus, it must be reserved in advance.
- Will students be eating lunch there? Do they bring a bag lunch, can they buy one there, or should I order a school lunch?
- What will the trip cost, per child? If this is too high for many families, will you have a bake sale to cover the cost, or will you provide scholarships? Can the PTA assist you financially?
- Do I need the principal's approval?
- What do I do if a child can't go?
- What do I do if permission slips or money aren't returned on time?
- Do the chaperones need to pay?
- Will chaperones be allowed to bring other siblings or family members?
- Write a permission slip and include a due date.

**Figure 4–4   Sample permission slip**

# Field Trip!

Dear Parents,

To conclude our science unit on insects, our class is going on a field trip to **the San Francisco Zoo**!! We will be traveling by school bus.

**Date**: Thursday, April 12
**Bus leaves school**: 9am
**Bus returns**: 2:30pm
**Cost**: $5.00 per child

Your child needs to bring:

\*A bag lunch
\*Good walking shoes
\*A light jacket
\*And, if they wish, a small amount of money for souvenirs

## We need chaperones!

If you are interested in joining us, please check the chaperone box below and include an additional $5 for your bus fare.

Thanks!


Ms. Heyda

Please return the bottom portion of this letter to me, with your child's $5 by **April 5**.

---

Child's Name _____

_____ yes, my child has permission to go to the San Francisco zoo on April 12th
_____ no, my child does not have permission
_____ I would like to chaperone, my name is _____

Total amount of money enclosed  $ _____

_____     _____
Parent Signature                                                              Date

*What Are Some Teaching Strategies and Activities I Can Use?*     • **69**

### A Week before the Trip

- Will the students travel as one group, or will they travel in small groups supervised by parents?
- Divide your students into partners or groups. If I have enough parents, I like to leave myself without a group so I can travel independently and visit with everyone.
- You may want to bring a snack for your students to eat when they arrive. It doesn't matter what time of day it is, young children always seem to be hungry when they arrive at their destination.
- Review the field trip rules several days in advance. For example, sit on your bottom in the bus, no running or screaming in the museum, and always stay close to your adult chaperone.
- Type up a field trip guide for your chaperones with all the pertinent information they need.
- Will your children have a list of things to look for, or questions to answer as they walk around? Will they need clipboards and pencils?
- Where will you store the lunches in the morning? Will the students carry them, will the chaperones carry them, are there lockers for food, or can you keep the food on the bus?
- Create student nametags in case a child gets lost. I prefer to print out self-stick nametags with the school's name, address, and phone number. I leave the child's name off for their safety and security.
- Create a plan B in case of rain, or unforeseen changes.

### On the Day of the Trip

- Be sure to carry bandages, emergency telephone numbers, and a cell phone if you have one.
- Allow the children to use the bathroom before you leave.
- Always count the children yourself because you are ultimately responsible for them.
- Bring a couple of garbage bags in case someone has motion sickness on the bus.
- Wear something bright or noticeable in case a child or parent needs to find you.
- Bring a camera and make a point of taking at least one picture of each child. Make two sets of photos. Put one set up on the wall for everyone to enjoy and give each student his or her photo so

**Figure 4–5   Sample chaperone guide**

# Chaperone Guide for the San Francisco Zoo!

**Chaperone Name** _____

**Number of children in your group** _____

**Student names** _____
_____
_____
_____
_____

## Today's schedule:

| | |
|---|---|
| 8:45am | Board the Bus |
| 9:00 | Bus leaves school |
| 9:30 | Bus arrives at the zoo |
| 9:40 | Explore the zoo! |
| 1:30pm | Meet by the north gate |
| 1:45 | Board the bus |
| 2:00 | Bus leaves the zoo |
| 2:30 | Bus arrives back at school |

**Lunch:** Eat whenever your students are hungry!

## Zoo Rules:

No running
No climbing on exhibits
Don't harass the animals
No screaming in zoo buildings
Students need to stay with their chaperone at all times

All students must visit the "Insect Zoo" as a follow up to our insect
unit.

Enjoy your Day!

the child can use it as a writing prompt, not to mention a souvenir of the experience.
- Take a deep breath, relax, and be flexible. Remember to have fun. Every time I take my students on a field trip we are bonded by the experience. Enjoy their excitement. Sometimes the bus ride is their favorite part of the trip. Everything will work out fine.
- Be flexible.

## Your Voice and Speaking Volume

You can use different volumes of voice to capture the attention of your students. Louder is not necessarily better. When I really want the children to listen, I talk very softly. A loud excited voice makes them energetic and jumpy.

## Closing a Lesson

How will you know if your students understood the lesson? This is an important key to effective teaching, yet it is easy to forget.

### Early Finishers

What will the children do if they finish their work early? I recommend you let them read in your class library, work on an on-going project, or keep a stack of independent work off to the side for your students to choose from.

### Assessment

One of the best ways to determine if your students comprehend the subject matter is to give them an assessment at the end of the unit or lesson. There may be an assessment built into the curriculum you are teaching. But if you do not have an assessment or want more information, you will need to create your own. Here are some ideas:

- watch students and listen to their discussions
- collect student work in a portfolio
- interview the students; ask them questions
- write what they know on the subject
- teach what they learned to another student, group, or class
- teacher-created multiple-choice tests
- teacher-created essay tests
- teacher-created fill-in-the-blank tests

*The Primary Teacher's Survival Guide*

Figure 4–6   Sample observation assessment

## Observation Assessment

Student Name _____          Date _____

**Subject:** Math
**Activity:** Building and Recording Block Patterns

**Can build on their partner's block pattern:**



**Can design an original block pattern:**



**Can record their block pattern on paper with 100% accuracy:**



**Strategies Observed:**



**Difficulties:**



**Other Observations:**

Figure 4–7    Sample interview assessment

## Interview Assessment

Student Name _____    Date _____

**Subject:** Science
**Unit:** Plants

What are the parts of a plant?


What do the roots and leaves do?


What is the reason for a flower?


What are the parts of a seed?


Name at least three ways a seed can travel.


What three things does a plant need to grow?


Explain the life cycle of a sunflower.


Name at least three uses for plants.


What else do you know about plants?

Figure 4–8    Sample essay test assessment

## Frogs

**Student Name** _____        **Date** _____

Describe the life cycle of the frog using words and/or pictures:

List at least five "froggy facts" learned in class:

Draw a picture of a frog and label its parts:

You design what is most helpful to you. I wanted to know if my 1st graders knew the names of all the coins and their values. I created a short test in which I asked them to match the picture of the coin with the name, and another in which they matched the name with the value. When I graded the tests I was disappointed with the results. Perhaps the pictures of the coins were not clear enough. I felt that the children should have done better so I tried something different. One at a time I called the kids aside, gave each of them a coin, and asked the child the value and name. I recorded their answers on a piece of paper and had a much clearer picture of what my students understood.

## *Questioning and Wait Time*

One way to assess if your students understand what you are teaching is to ask them questions. In fact, it is helpful to ask questions throughout your lesson to know if the students are following you and if you need to slow down and explain more. There is an art to questioning that only comes through practice. Consider asking open-ended questions that involve intellectual thought instead of predicted answers. Avoid yes or no questions. For example, "How do you think the story is going to end? Describe the main character of the story. Have you ever felt like the main character? Explain. What is a different way of solving the problem?"

Some students need more time to think about an answer before they raise their hands. I usually wait at least five seconds before calling on students or expecting an answer. Never force a child to answer. Response should be strictly voluntary. When a student answers a question incorrectly, acknowledge the answer and effort, and encourage further thought, help them work through the answer, or try a different approach.

# Homework

The purpose of homework is to reinforce skills learned in the classroom. Children often need to practice a new skill more than once before they are proficient.

## When to Assign

Some teachers assign homework on a daily basis. I prefer to send home a packet every Friday in a special homework folder.

You will need to think ahead of time and prepare the work at least a day in advance. I assign reading, math, and spelling homework for every night. The work goes home on Friday, and it is due back to me the following Friday. This practice gives the students the weekend to get started. I send the work home this way because in some households both parents work and the only time the children get to sit down and get help from their moms and dads is on the weekends. It also allows for flexibility in the student's work habits. Some children like to do their homework all at one time, others like to spread it out over the week, and others pull *all-nighters*.

## What to Assign

Homework should be a continuation and elaboration of what the children have learned in school.

Some homework ideas are presented here.

*The Primary Teacher's Survival Guide*

**Figure 4–9    Homework folder**

## Math Games Already Learned in Class

Our math curriculum contains a game called Ten's Go Fish. It is much like the card game Go Fish, except that students are using number cards from zero to ten and the goal is to make combinations of ten. For homework the children take home a copy of the number cards, play the game with a parent or sibling, and write about what happened in the game.

## Nightly Reading Assignments

The children are asked to read for twenty minutes a night. One night they are asked to record the book and write what it was about. Another night they read for twenty minutes and write about their favorite character. Other ideas are to ask them to describe the setting of the story, write their favorite part of the story, and describe the problem in the story and how that problem was solved.

### Spelling Practice

Ask the students to write their spelling words in alphabetical order, use each word in a sentence, write each word five times, write the dictionary definition of each word, and create a word search or crossword puzzle with their spelling words.

### Writing a Short Story or Essay

Relate the writing assignment to whatever theme you are teaching. If you are studying snow, ask them to write a story about snow. If you are reading pattern books such as Eric Carle's *Brown Bear, Brown Bear*, ask them to create their own, for example, "Ms. Heyda, Ms. Heyda, what do you see? I see a spider looking at me."

### Research

For example, when studying plants, ask the students to go home and look for seeds in the kitchen; the student should write the name of the seed and tape a sample to a paper. Find an article about weather in a newspaper or magazine, read it, and write what you learned.

### Story Problems

Send home an equation such as 8 + 11. Ask the students to write a story to fit the equation and solve the equation. For example, "Jack had 8 balloons, his brother gave him 11 more. How many balloons does Jack have now?" You can also make up your own problem and ask your students to solve it using at least two different strategies. Or assign a problem that will be different for everyone. For example, "Figure out how many legs are in your family, including pets."

### Computation Practice

This is basically a page full of math problems your students can solve independently at home.

### Reading a Poem Learned in Class

Every week I teach my students a song or poem. They take this home at the end of the week and read it to their families.

## Student Participation (Completion and Return)

Here are a few ways I encourage the completion and return of homework:

- I explain my expectations to the parents at back-to-school night.
- I explain the importance of homework to my students.
- I make the assignments clear enough so that the students can complete them on their own and always model how to do the work before sending it home.
- I reward the students with a sticker on their homework folder if completed on time.
- I make the assignments as interesting and as much fun as possible.
- If homework is incomplete, I either call or write a note to the parents.
- If homework is incomplete, I ask the students to finish it at recess.
- If homework is forgotten (and this happens on a regular basis), the child may lose her recess time.
- I send home an award saying, "Congratulations, you completed __ homework assignments on time!"

## Parent Participation

One way to involve the parents in helping their child with homework is to ask them to initial every assignment I give. Every homework packet has a coversheet recommending what should be completed each day. Next to the title of each assignment is a box for the parent and student to initial.

Another way to encourage parental involvement is to assign work that the child cannot do alone.

## Math games

The math game I explained in the section "Math Games Already Learned in Class" is a good one to use.

## Family Interviews

Students develop a list of questions in class, then go home and interview a family member. For example, during career week they can interview a family member about his or her job. What does the person do? What are the job responsibilities? What did he or she need to know before getting the job? What has the person learned from the job? What does he or she like best about the job?

**Figure 4–10   Homework cover sheet**

## Homework

Name: _____      Student

| | | |
|---|---|---|
| **Monday** | D.E.A.R.—Drop Everything and Read twenty minutes or more at your independent level. Write in reading journal.<br>Poem of the week—read and recite. | |
| | Math—do worksheet #1. | |
| | Spelling—write a sentence with five or more words. | |
| **Tuesday** | D.E.A.R.—Drop Everything and Read twenty minutes or more at your independent level. Write in reading journal.<br>Poem of the week—read and recite. | |
| | Math—do worksheet #2. | |
| | Spelling—do word search. | |
| **Wednesday** | D.E.A.R.—Drop Everything and Read twenty minutes or more at your independent level. Write in reading journal.<br>Poem of the week—read and recite. | |
| | Math—Price-a-word. | |
| | Spelling—Complete a-b-c order and price-a-word. | |
| **Thursday** | D.E.A.R.—Drop Everything and Read twenty minutes or more at your independent level. Write in reading journal.<br>Poem of the week—read and recite. | |
| | Math—do worksheet #3. | |
| | Spelling—Do special spelling sheet. Study for the test. | |

## I have checked to see that my child has completed their homework.

_____      _____

**Parent's/Guardian's Signature**                                    **Date**

**Figure 4–11    Diorama for *The Three Billy Goats Gruff***

## Creating a Diorama or Model

Let's say the entire class is reading the *Three Little Bears* in school. The children have discussed the story, written about it, acted it out, and drawn pictures of their favorite part. Extend the story to home. Send home a typed version of the story (unless you have a book for everyone) and instructions on how to make a diorama of their favorite scene. A diorama is a life-like three-dimensional model or scene, usually made in a shoebox sitting on its side.

## Grading Homework

I don't assign a grade to the homework when it is returned. Most parents look over their child's work and correct it with them. However, I do read and check everything. If the assignment is done correctly I put a star at the top of the paper. If there are mistakes I mark them as wrong and, when appropriate, write comments to help the student and parents better understand the assignment. Usually I take the homework home on the weekend and correct it when I can spare an hour. I make a huge effort not to let the grading get backed up because it can take a long time to catch up.

# Student of the Week

Once a week I celebrate the uniqueness of a student. It has nothing to do with academic achievement, test scores, or popularity. Every student gets a turn. I post a picture of the student in the middle of a big piece of construction paper. Around the student I place *bubbles* saying their birthday, favorite subject, favorite food, favorite color, favorite TV show, and what they want to be when they grow up. The picture is posted over a table specifically designated for the student. Every day that week the student is allowed to bring in an item from home for show-and-tell and leave it at school on the student-of-the-week table. I encourage photos, awards, and things they created themselves in place of toys. It is better if the item has a personal story to go along with it. At the end of the week they take everything home and I pull a name out of a basket to choose the next student.

# Show-and-Tell

Show-and-tell is an appropriate activity once a week for kindergarten and 1st grade. In 2nd and 3rd grade I recommend using it once a month, or as an award for good class behavior. In its simplest form, the children bring an item from home, tell their classmates about it as they sit in a circle, answer questions about the object, and pass it around for everyone to see and touch (as long as it isn't breakable). I set rules, such as, you need to listen if it is not your turn, ask thoughtful questions, be polite, treat each object with respect when handling it, and clap after each child's turn. If a student does not speak English, I try to find another student to translate. Bringing an item for show-and-tell is always optional, but everyone needs to participate by listening. I like to extend show-and-tell by asking the students to write down three clues about what their object is before hand and letting the students guess what it is before it is shown.

# Circle Time

An important part of the school day is circle time. This is when you gather the students in a circle for a classroom meeting or discussion. In the beginning of the school year I like to create a talking stick. The talking stick is a tool for facilitating discussion. Tribal communities throughout time have used it. Whoever holds the talking stick is the only person in the circle who can speak. Everyone else must give the talker their full attention and not interrupt. I create the talking stick with the class so they have ownership of it. Each child makes a bead out of self-hardening clay and paints it when it is dry. The beads are strung onto a piece of yarn or leather and tied around the stick. The stick can be passed from person to person or can be placed in the middle of the circle for the children to pick up when they're ready to speak. This is a great way to discuss sensitive issues like teasing, addiction, gang violence, and death. You can also pass the talking stick to solve problems such as tattling and lack of teamwork. The children can hold the talking stick and share their successes, failures, or just anything they feel like telling the group. Sharing is optional. Anyone can pass if they don't feel comfortable talking in front of the group.

# Second Language Learners

On my very first day of teaching I walked into my room five minutes before school started and noticed a girl quietly sitting at her desk. I went over to her and said, "Hello. What is your name?" She didn't answer, she just stared at me. "Are you Rosa?" I asked, noticing she was sitting at the desk with the nametag "Rosa." She smiled and nodded. I smiled back. "Welcome," I told her. "My name is Ms. Heyda." Then the bell rang.

After the children were settled in their seats I called for a volunteer to help. "Does anyone speak Spanish and English?" Several students raised their hands. I sat one of the girls who looked particularly friendly next to her. "Ask Rosa if she speaks any English." The girl asked and listened to a long answer. "No," she replied, "She only speaks Spanish and just moved here from Mexico yesterday." Several students volunteered to be Rosa's *buddy*, translate for her, and guide her around the campus.

This experience isn't unusual. Every year I have at least one or two students who speak no English at all and several who are limited English speakers. Here are some strategies you can use in the classroom to help facilitate their understanding.

- Even if you don't speak the language, welcome the child to your classroom with a big smile and a warm and friendly voice. Show the child around the classroom no matter what time of the year it is.
- Assign the student a buddy, preferably one who speaks the language, as I described, and who can translate for you.
- Carefully watch the language you use when speaking to the child. Don't talk baby talk or you will embarrass him; be careful not to speak extra loud, because he is not hearing impaired; and don't use difficult vocabulary unless you've taught the child the meaning first.
- Find out what English as a Second Language curriculum your school is using and implement it as soon as possible in your classroom.
- Be encouraging and positive. Don't put the child down for her mistakes. Make her feel welcome in your school.
- Use lots of visuals to get concepts across. Draw pictures next to key vocabulary words and use photos and diagrams whenever possible.
- Give the students hands-on experiences. If you are teaching about starfish, allow them to hold and examine a starfish. If you are teaching addition, teach them how to use manipulatives to solve a problem.
- Label the room. Write the names of all the important objects in your classroom on pieces of paper or sentence strips and tape them to the objects. For example, tape the word *door* on the door.

Teaching second language learners is an art. A lot of strategies and techniques, language acquisition theory, and studies have been done to help teachers. The strategies I've listed previously are the tip of the iceberg. Whole credentials are now devoted to teachers of second language learners. If you want to learn more, I recommend you find out what classes your local college or university has to offer and look at the following books:

*Working with Second Language Learners, Answers to Teachers' Top Ten Questions* by Stephen Cary, Heinemann, 2000
*Empowering Minority Students* by Jim Cummins, California Association for Bilingual Education, 1989
*Teaching Language Minority Students in the Multicultural Classroom* by Robin Scarcella, Prentice Hall Regents, 1990

# *Final Thoughts*

Part of the adventure of teaching is finding new and creative ways to reach your students. Be open to trying new strategies. Some will work for you, some won't. The funny thing about teaching techniques is that some will work with one class, but not the next. The strategies I've listed in this chapter should work with most students, but modifications will always be necessary to meet the diverse needs of such a diverse population of children. Have fun discovering your favorites.

# 5

# *How Do I Stay Organized?*

A coworker was helping me with a math lesson in my classroom one morning. I complained to her, "Look at my desk! It's a mess! I can't deal with it! I can't find anything I need! I can't even sit and work there!" To my disbelief she said that it was nothing. During one of her first years of teaching she had an even bigger pile of papers on her desk. One day the fire marshal came to school to inspect the building. When he got to her classroom and saw her desk he declared it a fire hazard. Now that's embarrassing! I had a clear vision of yellow tape wrapped around my desk saying, "Caution, fire hazard." This vision inspired me to ask myself, "What did my mess say about me? What kind of message was I sending to my students when I told them to clean their desks while mine was buried in papers?" Something needed to be done. I started by getting rid of my desk and getting organized. My desk supplies went into plastic utility drawers and the papers into files. Much of the mess on my desk had no value and ended up in the garbage.

Every year I have discovered new organizational techniques. Here they are.

## *The Everything Binder*

This is my secret weapon against disorganization. I never leave school without it. If a coworker can't find an important memo, chances are

**Figure 5–1   My everything binder**

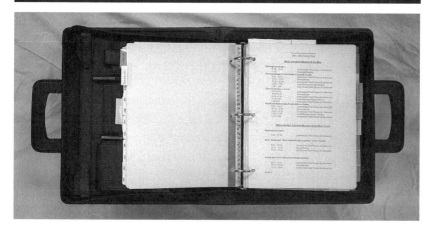

I've got it in my everything binder. No more shuffling through piles of papers on my desk, I have everything I need at my fingertips.

## Create Your Own Everything Binder

### Start with

A three-ring binder (preferably the kind that zips around the edges)
A three-hole punch

### Fillers (all three-hole punched)

At least ten paper dividers with tabs (preferably the kind with pockets)
Loose-leaf notebook paper
Lesson plan book
Grade book
A calendar
A pencil case

The following paragraphs explain the way my everything binder is organized. As you work with yours you will fine-tune it to suit your needs.

In my binder I have a pencil case with several pockets. In the pockets I keep all of my school receipts, stamps, computer disks with important teaching documents, and a spare sticky note pad for miscellaneous tasks.

*How Do I Stay Organized?*

The next thing I include is a handful of plain notebook paper. All are blank except for the top sheet, which contains the current date and my to-do lists. The to-do list is a very important tool for me. The act of putting everything I have to do in writing saves my brain from going over the list in my head over and over again. Once a thought is on the list I don't need to keep thinking about it. The list also helps me decide which task is most important. For example, if I need to create substitute lesson plans for the following day, I'm not going to clean out my file cabinet. My lists are titled "short-term school," "long-term school," "things to purchase for school," and lastly "home." Under each list I prioritize what is most important by drawing a star by those items. As the day goes on I constantly refer to this list, crossing out and adding things as I go. At the end of the day I tear out my list and rewrite a new one with the unfinished items.

My lesson plans come next (which I write in a spiral lined notebook), then my grade book and calendar of school events.

The last section of my notebook contains dividers with tabs. I organize my paperwork under the following categories:

Current: weekly memos, upcoming field trips, and articles I need to read . . .

Schedules: school schedule, PE, music, library, computer lab, speech . . .

Phone numbers: student/parent numbers, staff numbers, phone trees, volunteers . . .

Class lists: several copies of my current class list, reading class list . . .

Forms: supply orders, publication department orders . . .

Committees: duties, projects in progress, records of meetings . . .

Professional development: list of the workshops and classes I've attended, certificates, units . . .

Generic subplans: Subplans I can fax to the school if I am too ill to come to class

Miscellaneous: Anything that doesn't fit the previously listed categories

Any paperwork I need to keep goes under one of these files. I try to update my files every day, but if I don't have time I can just zip new papers into the binder until I have time to organize them. When I can

1-28-02

Priority
* Photocopy & staple homework
  Grade spelling test
* Call Nancy's Parents
  Call in book orders
  write next weeks lesson plans

Later
Write emergency sub plans
file assessments
organize math
   materials
clean fish tank
update bulletin board

Home
* Pay bills
  Laundry
* Call mom

* = top priority

no longer zip the binder closed or my arms are sore from carrying its weight, I know it is time for a spring cleaning.

# Keeping Up with Paperwork

Teachers are so busy! One of the hardest things to do is just to keep up with all the paperwork and cleaning up. When I get swamped, things pile up and eventually I need to stay at school late or go in on a weekend to clean up the mess.

An easy way to keep on top of paperwork and messes is to set aside a time of day, every day, for cleaning. For me, this is usually right after school. Usually cleanup only takes fifteen to thirty minutes. The work pays off because I love coming into my classroom in the morning and finding it neat and organized. I have learned that when my classroom is clean I feel more relaxed and do a better job of teaching.

# Curriculum and Teaching Books

Keep your curriculum organized. I always know where to go to find my math or spelling books. It helps to have lots of bookshelves. For example, I keep all my literacy books right behind my chair at the reading table. If a student asks a question I can't answer or a teachable moment comes up, I can turn around and find the resource I need.

After you teach a lesson, put your notes, comments, and reflections on sticky note pads and attach them to the lesson. When you go to teach the same thing next year, you can refer back to your notes and make any necessary changes. This saves a lot of time and frustration. Believe me, I've learned the hard way.

# Units

I started organizing my units in my first year. As a 1st grade teacher I found it hard to store my teaching materials in traditional files. The art projects and decorations just didn't fit inside them. Instead, I collected the cardboard boxes that hold copy paper. If you have a large enough school budget, you might choose to buy plastic storage containers at discount stores. I labeled each box with the month and stored it on a shelf. Later, I expanded my box collection to include language arts, math, oceans, insects, and other subjects.

# Materials to Help You Get Organized

* baggies (all sizes; the two-gallon size is the best because 8½" × 11" paper fits inside)
* copy paper boxes: you should be able to find these in your copy room
* plastic tubs, like the kind you use for washing dishes

**Figure 5–3   Monthly theme units**

* shoe boxes from all the new shoes you wear out walking around in your classroom

In the beginning I threw all the black line masters, samples of student work, and lesson plans into the boxes in one big jumble. By my second year I found it very hard to find anything I needed. Something needed to be done. Slowly, as I found the time, I put the paperwork in plastic sleeves for safekeeping, then into three-ring binders. The binders are organized like the boxes, by month and subject. Only keep one copy of each worksheet or handout. Recycle the rest. It just isn't practical to count what you saved next year, subtract that number from what you actually need, and then make copies. Trust me, I tried it.

# Filing

## Files for the File Cabinet

You will need to make binders and files to organize your paperwork all year long. The most important files you create are for your students. As soon as you know who your students are, create files for them. These files should be in an easily accessible place since they will be in continuous use. Fill them with late slips, student writing, communication from parents, and anything else you need to document.

Other files might include emergency cards, field trip permission slips, class photos, book orders, letters from students (I call it fan mail), catalogs, and forms or worksheets that you use in large quantities throughout the year.

It can be helpful to have a special binder for staff meetings. In my school all the teachers are given a binder to bring to meetings and store all the papers we receive.

## Computer Files

I use my computer frequently at school. It is wonderful for typing up homework, a class poem, substitute lesson plans, letters to parents, report card comments, and field trip notices. Be sure to file your documents all in one place. Organize it much like you would a traditional file cabinet. Routinely save your work to a back-up disk, especially if you let your students use your computer.

## Test Results

I like to file test results separately from student work. Having all the assessments in one place makes it easier for me to analyze student progress and establish report card grades. I still use the grade book for some assessments such as spelling tests, but I find I need to look at the actual test protocol to accurately assess a child's understanding and difficulties. I organize test results in a three-ring binder. I write each child's name on a tabbed divider and file their assessments behind their name.

*The Primary Teacher's Survival Guide*

**Figure 5–4  Sample schedule**

## Terrific Tuesday
## Regular Day

| | |
|---|---|
| 8:25 | Attendance/Lunch Count |
| 8:30 | Poetry |
| 8:45 | Reading Switch |
| 8:50 | Reading Group A |
| 9:30 | Reading Group B |
| 10:10 | Recess |
| 10:30 | Spelling |
| 10:45 | Calendar |
| 11:00 | Math |
| 12:00 | Lunch |
| 1:00 | DEAR Time |
| 1:25 | Literature |
| 2:00 | Science |
| 2:35 | Student Jobs/Clean Up |
| 2:45 | Dismissal |

# Teacher Routines

Establishing routines in the classroom is vital to accomplishing all the many tasks teachers do. Your first year will be trial and error, finding what works for you. Here are some of the things I do. I hope they will give you some ideas and get you started.

## Before School

I usually get to school an hour or more before school starts so I can beat the heavy morning traffic from San Francisco to San Mateo. I hope this is not the case for you. Anyway, after I open the classroom door and set down my bags I head straight for the coffee maker. While a good strong cup is brewing I turn on the classical music station and my Zen water fountain, check my email and voice mail, water the plants, and feed the fish. I gather any papers I need to copy and head off for the copy room with coffee in hand. While I'm out, I empty my mailbox and deliver notes or memos.  Then it's back to my classroom where I check the to-do list in my everything binder, change the calendar, write the schedule for the day on the whiteboard, and gather together all the materials I need for teaching that day. The bell rings and the day begins.

### During School

During the school day I do my best to stay on top of putting away teaching materials and papers after I use them. On days when I have planning time I grade papers, copy homework for the week ahead, and update my files. Some days can be very hectic. I don't pressure myself to accomplish any tasks outside of teaching when I'm having a busy day. Everything I don't have time for goes on the to-do list.

### After School

After the kids leave I clean up paperwork, lessons, and the occasional student messes. This is usually the time I work on larger projects such as creating new literacy centers, inventing activities, changing bulletin boards, filling book orders, laminating student work, reorganizing the class library, and grading papers. I make an effort not to stay after school longer than an hour (see Chapter 7, How Do I Teach and Still Have a Life?), but that is difficult when there is so much to do.

# Writing Lesson Plans

I don't always have time to write my lesson plans at school. Some weekends I bring home my teacher guides and lesson plan book. This was especially necessary my first year of teaching, when I changed grade levels, and when the district adopted a new curriculum. I base my planning on the curriculum guides, the state and district standards, student assessment results (formal and informal), and my own vision of what I want to accomplish over the year. It only takes me an hour or so to sit down and decide what I will do for the week ahead. The comfort of my own home makes it easier for me to think about the purpose of my lessons and how I will teach them. Planning for the week ahead also gives me a feeling of security that I am ready to teach on Monday morning. At school, I lay out everything I need for the week on a big table.

*The Primary Teacher's Survival Guide*

## Figure 5–5 Lesson plan book

GRADE OR CLASS _____

| Subject | MONDAY Jan 6 | TUESDAY Jan 7 | WEDNESDAY Jan 8 |
|---|---|---|---|
| 8:15–8:45 | Schedule / Attendance / Lunch Count / New Student Jobs / Introduce Song – "You Are My Sunshine" | → read song w/ hand motions | → sing song with tape → |
| 8:45–10:10 | Reading Switch → (introduce bl blend words) | → ↓ (introduce cl blend words) | → ↓ (introduce fl blend words) |
| recess | → | → | → |
| 12:00 | Spelling–introduce new words / Calendar | PE – 10:30–11:00 / Music – 11:05–11:35 | Spelling – review challenge words / Calendar |
| 10:30 | Math – adding 10's (review place value) | Spelling – vocabulary definitions | Math – (review adding by 10's) introduce multiplying by 10's |
| lunch | → | → | → |
| 12:00 | DEAR Time → Literature – "Six Dinner Sid" picture walk, read, discuss / Science–introduce weather journal / Student Jobs → / Dismissal → | Literature/Writing – "What Will Six Dinner Sid do next?" / Science – introduce temperature / Pass out Tuesday envelopes → | 12:35 Dismissal |

# Long-Term Planning

Long-term planning is important for setting goals and meeting standards but difficult to do as a first-year teacher. You are so busy with so many new things it is difficult to look more than a week ahead. A simple way to start is with your curriculum guides. Write down the

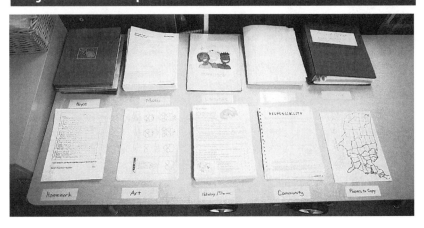

**Figure 5–6    Lesson plan table**

main themes, skills, and subjects that are covered throughout the year. Spread them out over the months you are teaching. Cross-reference your plan with your state's teaching standards. Note which standards are not represented in your curriculum and insert them where they are most appropriate. For example, don't introduce algebra before addition. Share your plan with a seasoned teacher, preferably at your grade level, and ask for feedback. Perhaps the teacher has a long-term plan he or she can share with you. Use your long-term plan as a guide for your weekly lessons. Remember, nothing is written in stone, your students will learn some skills faster than others, and it is unlikely that you will accomplish everything you set out to do by the end of the year.

## *Final Thoughts*

Everything has its place. That's my motto. When my room is clear of clutter, I can think clearer, I'm more relaxed, and my students are happier. It doesn't take long to learn that good organization saves time and energy. And in this job you need all the time and energy you can get.

# How Do I Prepare for ...?

The end of my first year of teaching was a month away. I could almost taste my freedom. After a long busy year, I was ready to rest, reflect, and do something special for myself. I started to notice I was feeling crabby and impatient, my students were having more discipline problems than usual, and my coworkers were getting grumpier each day. One afternoon I met with my grade level team. "I'm finished with my cume folders!" one of them exclaimed. "I'm almost finished with the benchmark testing!" said a second. "My student ID cards are complete!" reported the last teacher. "What are all of you talking about?" I asked. They read me the list of tasks I was to complete by the last day of school. I was stunned. I had no idea there was so much paperwork to do. It seemed to me the most intense work of the school year was at the very end. At least now I knew why my coworkers were grumpy. The countdown was on.

In this chapter I help to prepare you for some of the bigger events of the school year. You won't be caught by surprise like me. I've put the events in the order I think you will need them, starting with back-to-school night and ending with the last days of school.

## Back-to-School Night

Back-to-school night is the time when the parents of your students come to school to meet you and hear you talk about the grade level or program their child is enrolled in. I remember being very nervous before my first back-to-school night. I didn't know what to expect, and being brand new I didn't feel qualified to talk about the program since I was just learning it myself. This chapter should leave you better prepared than I was.

## The Week Before

It is not necessary to do anything elaborate with the classroom. School has only been in session for a few weeks and there hasn't been time to display student work and make special decorations. Just make sure your room is reasonably neat and clean.

A few days before, ask the students to make invitations for their parents. Explain to them how important it is that their parents come.

Prepare a sign-in sheet for the parents to write their name and their child's name.

Also, prepare a sign-in sheet for conferences. Many parents will ask you how their child is doing in class, which is not the purpose of back-to-school night. Tell them politely that to properly answer their questions you need to sit down and look at their child's work. Invite them to come in for a conference and refer them to the conference sign-in sheet.

### Notes and Points to Get Across

Make an outline of the information you want to get across, preferably a week in advance. This is to give yourself time to think about what you want to say and add anything you may have forgotten. Here are some of the things I include in my notes:

* my name
* my experience as a teacher
* the class schedule (generic)
* classroom rules, awards, consequences
* what their child needs to bring to school
* summary of the different programs
* the skills their child will learn in different subject areas
* any big themes I have planned, for example, oceans
* upcoming field trips
* an example of end of the year reading level
* an example of end of the year writing

* homework expectations
* basics on helping their child with reading at home
* your school phone number and email address
* list of supplies that the class needs

This may seem like a lot, but most of the points listed take little time to explain.

## Handouts

I prepare a packet of handouts for the parents ahead of time. In this packet I include the following items:

* the district's language arts and math standards
* a general class schedule, including library, PE, computer lab, and music
* a student information sheet for the parents to fill out
* a sign-up sheet for volunteers
* a list of supplies that are needed
* my school phone number and email address
* what their child needs to bring to school
* my classroom rules and discipline plan
* any current handout or newsletter on how parents can support their child's learning at home

Make a transparency of every handout. Project them on a wall or screen with an overhead projector to make it easier for the parents to follow along.

## Making Parents Feel Welcome

Greet the parents as they walk in the door. Direct them to sign in, take a handout packet, and find a seat. Don't wait more than five minutes for parents who are late; you want to leave enough time to explain everything on your agenda.

It's nice to provide snacks like pretzels or chips and juice. Put a basketful on every table and encourage your visitors to help themselves. Food can help put everyone at ease.

If any of your students are there that evening, choose one to volunteer as a supply model. When you explain all the supplies the students will need, ask the model to stand up and show off their backpack, crayons, lunch box, and so on. This should liven up the audience and put a smile on everyone's face.

## What to Expect

Introduce yourself and walk the parents through your handouts. Be sure not to miss anything in your notes. Visuals help make the talk more interesting. Show your transparencies. When you are finished, take a few questions. If you don't know the answer, be honest, write down the parents' name and question, and tell them you'll get back to them. Give each parent a piece of paper and ask him or her to write something they'd like you to know about their child. Remind the parents to sign up for a conference on their way out. This will make scheduling easier for you when conference time rolls around. Give yourself a pat on the back. You survived your first back-to-school night!

# Parent Conferences

Your district will most likely require you to hold at least one parent/ teacher conference a year. For those students who are learning below grade level or having other problems more may be necessary.

It is up to you to decide if you would like the student to be present at the conference. This can be a way to facilitate communication between parent, child, and teacher. You can increase the child's self-esteem by praising her in front of her parents. Instead of you doing all the talking, ask your student to share his writing and work with his family. Being part of the discussion of how to change that behavior may help children with behavior difficulties.

## Setting up Conferences

I hope you were able to schedule meetings with most of the parents when they came to back-to-school night. There are several different ways to schedule the others. Make phone calls. This is the easiest way to make sure you are setting a time that will work for everyone involved. Then, send a note home with the child confirming the day and time. If you can't reach the parent by phone, set a time that is good for you. Then send home a note stating the date and time you have scheduled and re-

*The Primary Teacher's Survival Guide*

quest a signature to confirm. If the date does not work, ask for suggestions for some another time. Coordinate conference times with other teachers who have siblings in their classrooms. If the parents do not speak English you will need to find out if there is a translator available at your school who can call for you or use a computer translation program to write your notes home. I recommend: Easy Translator (CD-ROM).

### Time Allotment

Schedule your conferences for twenty to thirty minutes. If you are meeting parents back-to-back, be sure to leave a ten-minute period in between for a short break or to compensate for parents who arrive late or need extra time to talk with you. Set up a waiting area outside your classroom for parents who arrive early or need to wait because you are running behind schedule. A couple of comfortable chairs and a small table with a parenting magazine for them to read works well.

### What Student Work to Show

Pull a sampling of student work from different subject areas. A couple of writing samples, math assignments, science investigations, and any assessments you have given. Keep on hand any notes you have on his behavior, attendance, homework, and a book he has read recently. If there are any permission slips or forms the parent needs to sign, keep those on hand.

### How to Talk with Parents

Always start with a warm welcome and introductions. It is professional practice to shake the hands of the parents before you sit down and begin the conference. Begin your meeting on a positive note. Tell the parents all the wonderful talents and qualities their child has. Even if this is a difficult student, everyone has inherent gifts. Remember to listen attentively, don't interrupt or talk over parents, and avoid educational terms that only a teacher could understand.

You can also start the conference by simply asking, "Tell me about your child . . . ."

Your follow-up questions might be:

* Is there anything I can clarify?
* How is the homework coming along?
* Is there a quiet work area at home?

* Is the child reading to you every night?
* What is the child's behavior like at home?
* If the child seems tired in the morning ask if she is getting enough sleep at night.

My current school policy is to schedule conference time when report cards go out. Our conferences center around explaining the report cards and the grades I've given. If this is not the case for you, focus on the subject areas, behavior, and anything else that might be an issue for you. Show the work samples you pulled and discuss areas in which the child is succeeding and in which improvement is needed. Explain whether the child is at grade level in that subject, and if not, what the parent can do to help at home.

Sometimes parents are difficult to talk with for a variety of reasons. Always remember to be patient, tolerant, and most of all compassionate. In the rare case of verbal or physical assault, call the office for help immediately. If you have concerns about a parent before scheduling the conference, don't schedule the parent to come after hours, or pick an evening when many of your coworkers have agreed to stay late too, just in case you need help.

You may want to teach some techniques for helping their child at home. For example, if the student is having difficulty adding and subtracting numbers, show the parents how you use manipulatives such as beans, a number line, tally marks, or fingers to solve problems. If the child is struggling with reading comprehension, give the parents examples of questions they can ask the child when the child finishes reading.

Before you finish, be sure to ask the parents if they have any questions for you. You may want to finish by reiterating any important points you want them to walk away with.

After the parents leave, write down any important notes you need to remember such as how you are going to follow-up the conference, any questions you could not answer, and concerns about the child or family.

# Report Cards

You will need to score report cards on a quarterly or trimester system. The most difficult and time-consuming report card is the first. This is because you have only just gotten to know your students and you are deciding where they are according to grade level standards. Subsequent report cards are easier because you already have a sense of how the child is performing academically. This makes it easier for you to diagnose the degree of her improvement.

One way to better prepare your students and help them understand their report card is to give them a blank copy. Then, make a transparent copy for the overhead projector and discuss each item line by line so they understand what they will be graded on.

## Looking at Student Work

As with parent/teacher conferences, collect examples of the students' work and assessments from the subject areas you will be grading them on. Check with your coworkers to find out if your school has guidelines or a rubric for grading student work. If not, I recommend sitting down with your fellow grade level teachers and asking them to share with you what they are doing. Whenever possible, grading should be consistent. Unfortunately, not all schools use a consistent grading plan.

Student self-evaluation is also a useful strategy. Learning begins with self-awareness and reflection. Create a rubric with the class. For example, if you are creating a writing rubric, ask the students what they feel is a great paper, a good paper, an okay paper, and a poor paper. Ask them to look at what they feel is their best writing and score it on the rubric they created. Let them talk with each other and you about why they feel they deserve this score and what they can do to improve the next time they write.

If you are not discussing grading with your grade level team, remember you need to back up every report card with the evidence to justify the grades. In most cases your grades will not be challenged, but it is best to be prepared just in case.

## Writing Report Card Comments

The comment section of the report card is for clarifying and elaborating on the grades. The following items are:

* a brief explanation of the child's grade
* areas of success
* areas that need the most work
* what the child needs to do to improve the grade

* behavior difficulties
* personality attributes
* motivation
* the pleasure they take in work
* day-dreaming, social interaction, and friendliness
* work habits
* how the child has adjusted to the school or your class
* why you enjoy having the child in your class
* number of completed homework assignments
* average spelling score

Of course, usually the comment section is very small and you won't have the space to write about all the areas mentioned previously. Choose the points that are the most important to get across and let the rest go. I make an effort to keep my comments positive even when behavior or skills are challenging. For example, "David is working on focusing his attention on his studies instead of socializing during seat work." Or, "Sarah's imaginative stories would be easier to read if she added spaces between her words." Discuss serious problems with the parents before putting them on the report card; everything you record goes into their permanent file.

# Open House

Open house is an event held later in the school year, often April or May. Students and parents are invited to come to school in the evening to look at all the work they have done and celebrate their success.

I love open house. I remember being really worried about it as I was before back-to-school night. When the evening started I had a great time. It was really fun to visit casually with my students and their families and show off the classroom.

## Preparation

Unlike back-to-school night you will want to do extra work to make sure your classroom looks its best. Start preparing several weeks before the big night.

*The Primary Teacher's Survival Guide*

Look at your current bulletin boards. If the work on them is outdated, and by outdated I mean if your students' work has improved since the display was created or it reflects a unit you taught three months ago, take it down. Your bulletin boards should reflect current work. Create at least one math, writing, science, and literature display filled with student creations. If you teach social studies, that should be reflected on the walls too. Some teachers tend to focus too much on art projects. Art is important, but the parents tend to be more concerned with the core curriculum. If your room is small like mine and you run out of wall space you can always post things on the chalkboard.

The reason I suggest starting work on open house several weeks in advance is because you might not have student work worthy of going up for the big night. There is still time for the children to write a great story or create a diorama of *The Three Little Pigs.*

If your classroom has become cluttered, start organizing. Sometimes teachers just run out of time for cleaning. Don't worry. I've learned from coworkers that a last minute mural on a large piece of butcher paper or some colorful fabric will hide a pile of sins. If things look really bad, you can always load the mess into the trunk of your car. But wouldn't you feel better if your classroom looked great because it was really organized?

Gather together all the student work you want to send home. I like to take a large sheet of construction paper, fold it in half, staple the sides, and voila, you have a folder. If there is enough time, the students can decorate them. Put all the papers inside so the families can carry their work home easily.

A few days before the big night ask your students to make invitations for their parents. And then ask them to bring a snack to share. The greater the turnout, the more fun everyone has.

Create a sign-in sheet for the parents to sign their names.

### Students as Tour Guides

I like to make my students into open house tour guides. A few days before, I create a check-off sheet of everything I'd like the parents to see and do while in the classroom. Then I share this tour guide with the students. I pretend to be a student and show them how I would use the guide to show my parents everything in the room. In the end the parent and child sign the sheet and return it to me. It works wonderfully. Instead of me talking all night, the students do the work. The children feel good about themselves and I can relax. Here is a partial tour guide:

### Room 31 Open House Tour Guide 2003

__ Introduce your parents to Ms. Heyda
__ Introduce your parents to a new friend
__ Visit the writing wall, find your story, and read it to your parents
__ Visit the math wall, find your paper, and explain to your parents how you solved the problem
__ Go to the class library and read your parents a story
__ Visit the ocean center and explain everything you learned about starfish
__ Look through the work in your take-home folder
__ Sign the bottom and return this sheet to Ms. Heyda

I've gotten really nice feedback from the parents when I have used the tour guide. One family told me that the year before they really didn't know what to look at in their child's room. They found themselves standing around feeling slightly uncomfortable. In my room they liked that the guide kept them busy and they got to see everything.

### Setup

On the day of open house make sure all of your bulletin boards are up. Ask the students to help prepare by washing desks and chairs, cleaning the inside of their desks and cubbies, and leaving their work envelopes on top of their desk at the end of the day. Set up a snack table. Create a table for signing in and picking up a tour guide. Take a deep breath. The hard part is over.

# Substitute Lesson Plans

Whether you call in sick, or go to a workshop or a meeting, at some point you will need to call for a substitute teacher. I substitute taught for a year and a half. In that time I went to many kindergarten through 5th grade classrooms. Every experience was different, some great, some extremely challenging. As a regular classroom teacher I reflect on those days as a substitute. I remember what was helpful for me and create my lesson plans drawing on my most positive experiences.

## Vital Information to Include

Here is some important information to include in your plans:

* a welcome note
* the time school starts
* how and where the kids line up in the morning, after recess, and after lunch
* what the kids are expected to do when they first come in
* any nicknames the kids prefer to be called; you can note this on the attendance sheet
* a reminder that you are collecting permission slips or anything else from home
* the times all lessons begin and end; be sure to allow time for cleanup
* detailed teaching instructions
* transitions; for example, explain how the kids get from the floor to the rug
* student jobs
* names and times students are pulled out for special classes
* who to ask if the substitute has a question
* procedures for the bathroom, drinks, and sharpening pencils
* classroom rules and your discipline techniques
* location of the nearest bathroom and the staff room
* notes on students with any special needs
* what to do with completed work
* the names of students who are the most helpful
* a class list
* a seating chart
* fire drill procedures
* school map
* your home phone number
* permission to change the plans as the substitute sees fit

Make sure you have gathered all the materials she will need, or leave detailed notes telling her where to find these things. Put all the materials for the day in one central location. I like to type out the plans on the computer so that they are easy to read. Keep the lessons simple. Put the substitute folder on your desk or in a place where it can be found easily.

## Generic Lesson Plans

There might be a day when you are too ill to come to school to prepare substitute plans. If you have created generic lesson plans and stored them where they can be easily found you won't need to worry.

Type up your plans like I described previously, only this time leave out the specific lessons. Instead, write the name of the subject and "see worksheets." Worksheets are not always the ideal way to teach, but when you are too ill to come in and plan something more enriching, they do the job. You may also need to type up different lesson plans for different days. For example, my Monday schedule was totally different from my Tuesday schedule. Put all of your lesson plans in a folder titled "generic lesson plans."

Make class sets of worksheets for the subjects you teach. The more the better. Place them in folders titled "math," "literature," etc. Find a central place to store your worksheets and plans. I have a space above the student cubbies labeled "guest teacher."

Here are some simple activities for your substitute:

* worksheets as I described previously
* DEAR (drop everything and read) time; students choose a couple of books and read quietly for a period of time
* read a story
* journal writing
* a movie
* free choice inside or outside

When you call in sick, instruct your substitute where to find these folders and to use the generic lesson plans you have created. Relax and heal, everything will work out fine in your absence.

Here is one of my emergency lesson plans.

## Tuesday Emergency Lesson Plans

Welcome! Thank you for teaching my class today! They are a wonderful group of twenty. I'm so sorry I couldn't create better plans for you. If you are reading this, I am out due to a severe emergency, or I'm really sick. :-(

Jane and John are reliable and helpful students and can answer some of your questions.

Please take out the brown wood coat rack (near the door) and hang it on the nails below the window outside.

If I was absent the day before, please change the date on the white board and adjust the schedule (magnets are in a cubbie next to the white board).

### 8:20 to 8:25

After the bell rings the students line up in front of the classroom, next to the redwood tree. Invite them in; they will go directly to their seats.

### 8:25 to 8:30

Introduce yourself. Review the date and schedule for the day (on the white board). Call the students by table to sit on the rug. You sit on the couch and take the attendance and lunch count. The job wheel can be found on the wall next to the door by the aquarium, if you need it. The messengers may take the attendance to the office.

### 8:30 to 8:35

Poetry: Read the poem of the week on the chart next to the couch all together. Call on students to make up hand motions to express each line of the poem. When you have a motion for each, practice reading the poem at least two times with all the hand motions.

### 8:35 to 8:40

Check the job wheel to see who passes out the jump ropes and balls and let them do their job.

### 8:40 to 8:45

Reading switch: Dismiss the students to their reading classes (the list of where they go is next to the door if you need it). A few students stay with you and go to their seats. Children from other classes come to you. Altogether you will have sixteen. Introduce yourself again.

**Figure 6–1  Guest teacher cubbies**

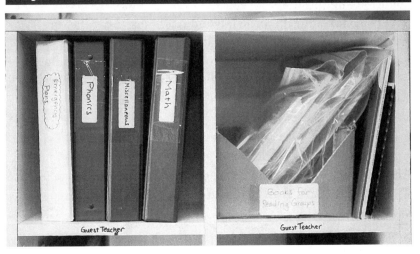

The students are divided into two reading groups, orange and yellow. The list of names can be found behind the kidney-shaped table on the white board.

Review the center rules with the whole class (on the far right panel white board).

### 8:45 to 9:25

Call the orange group to the reading table and ask the yellow group to go to their centers. The kids are well trained and know exactly what to do.

Behind the teacher's chair (below the white board) are two peach-colored tubs. One has an orange card on the front, and the other, a yellow card. Remove the zippable storage baggies from the orange tub and pass them out to the children. They read the stories inside for five minutes. You may time them if you wish.

After five minutes, collect the bags. Bring their attention to the pocket chart. Set the timer for one minute. As you point to the words the children read them (without your help). If they make a mistake, ask them to read the word again. Record the number of words read per minute on the white board under their color group. Repeat the activity, encouraging them to beat the previous number of words.

Introduce one of the stories in the Guest Teacher cubbie. If you had a chance to look at the book before school started, summarize what the story is about and go over any difficult vocabulary. Give each child a book. Give them a couple of minutes to look through it on their own. Then, echo read the story (you read a sentence, they repeat). Read the story again, this time everyone reads together with your help. Read the story a third time; this time you listen to the group read without you. Afterward, ask any questions that seem appropriate to check for understanding. Collect the books.

Worksheets (see file in "Guest Teacher" cubbie)

Collect all papers for me when finished.

### 9:25 to 9:30

Freeze the children by flipping the rainstick behind my chair. Instruct them to clean up and return to their seats.

### 9:30 to 10:05

Switch the groups. Call the yellow group to the reading table and send the orange group to centers. Repeat the previous activity.

### 10:05 to 10:10

Freeze the students again and clean up. If you finished both lessons early and have extra time, read them a story in the library.

### 10:10

Dismiss the children for recess.

### 10:10 to 10:30

Recess: In case of a rainy day, you need to keep the kids in the classroom. They can choose to draw or play with the toys or blocks, but not the computers.

### 10:30 to 11:00

PE : Meet the students outside. Ask any kids with balls and jump ropes to return them to the classroom, then ask the line leader to lead the class to PE.

***11:00 to 11:10***

Spelling: Refer to the spelling list on the far right panel of the white board. Pretend to throw each word to the students (only do this with the first ten words); they will catch it, repeat it, and fingerspell it. You can also play spelling scramble. Write a scrambled spelling word on the white board, ask for a student to identify it and spell it for you the correct way.

***11:10 to 11:30***

Calendar: Call the students to the rug by the table. Ask them to face the calendar. You have a choice of pointers on the floor next to the bookshelf. All markers and other materials you may need are in the storage box on the bookshelf. This is a regular routine for the children; they understand what to do and will help you.

* Sing the days of the week song ("Happy Days") as you point to the days of the week
* Read "yesterday was . . . today is . . . tomorrow will be . . ." as you point.
* Read the full date, for example "Today is Monday, December 10, 2001," as you point.
* Add the number of days we've been in school to the number strip.
* Add a straw to the place value pocket and correct the numbers above them.
* Add a tally mark to the monthly tally.
* Make today's date with coins.
* Fill in a square on the weather graph.
* Write as many equations as they can think of for the day's date.

***11:30 to 11:55***

Math: See worksheets in Guest Teacher cubbie. You choose what to do.

***11:55 to 12:00***

Pass out the lunch cards (they are next to the boom box in the library). The ball monitor and jump rope monitor do their jobs. The children line up by the door. You need to walk them to the lunch line.

In case of a rainy day, walk the kids to the gymnasium. They will watch a movie there while you eat your lunch. Return at 12:30 to walk them back to class (those buying lunch get into the lunch line) to eat their lunch inside under your supervision. If they finish eating early they can do the activities mentioned under rainy day recess.

### 1:00 to 1:20

Meet the children outside the classroom and walk them in. After they sit in their seats, call them by table to get a drink of water and choose two books to read at their desk for DEAR (drop everything and read) time. Ask them to read quietly to themselves. It is important for them to see you reading too! If their table has done a good job, give them a table point on the white board. Call the kids by tables to return their books and get their journals from their cubbies.

### 1:20 to 2:00

Writing: You can either ask the children to write about anything they want or give them a prompt. For example, "I looked to the night sky and saw . . . ."

### 2:00 to 2:35

Video: Choose a video from the shelf under the TV. Turn on the TV and VCR and slip the tape in. Don't handle the remote; every time I use it I end up having problems with it, so bad that we can't watch the movie sometimes. Trust me! Save yourself the frustration and adjust the sound, etc. manually.

### 2:35 to 2:45

Clean up! Students do their assigned jobs; others clean the tops of their desks and their baskets.

Pass out the Tuesday envelopes (in the basket under the little desk by the door) and all the papers to be sent home (in the desk by the door). If a child does not have his envelope, just staple the papers together for him.

If you have extra time, ask them to tell you what they remember doing in school today.

Make sure all students put their chairs up.

### 2:45

Dismissal

Please remember to bring in the coat rack so it will not be vandalized at night.

Please feel free to change these plans as you see fit.

Let me know of any discipline problems.

## Preparing Your Students

I always let my students know when I will be away from class. For some of them it can be scary and traumatic to come into class in the morning and find that someone else is in my place. They may feel uncomfortable because they don't feel safe. The regular routines are often different because the substitute teacher doesn't do things the same way I do. So, the day before, I talk to them about how tomorrow will be different. I give them a preview of the lessons I have planned for them. I always refer to the substitute as a guest teacher. This is not just any person filling in; this person is the teacher for the day to whom I've given control of the classroom. The guest teacher deserves to be respected as the authority. And, of course, I remind them that the guest teacher will write me a report at the end of the day, letting me know how things went. If anyone had difficulty behaving, there will be a consequence when I return. I encourage the kids to have fun and enjoy getting to know someone new. Their guest teacher has talents and gifts to share with them. It will be an adventure.

# Birthday Celebrations

I choose to handle student birthdays in a simple manner. Everyone sings "Happy Birthday." Then each of their classmates makes the child a birthday letter, saying at least one positive thing about him or her and illustrating it with thought and care. While the children are writing, the birthday boy or girl colors a construction paper folder in which I later staple the letters. At the end of the day they have a personal birthday book. Kindergarten children enjoy wearing a birthday crown for the day. If a student has a summer birthday, we celebrate their *half* birthday, so they have the experience of celebrating at school like the rest of their classmates. The birthday boy or girl is welcome to bring in cupcakes or cookies to share with classmates at recess time. I don't host large birthday parties because they take up vital learning time and may make other children feel bad if their parents cannot do the same for them.

# *Class Parties*

A few times a year I let my students have a class party. This is usually for Halloween; Christmas, Hanukkah, and Kwanzaa (celebrated together); Valentine's Day; and the last day of school. The more my room parent is willing to do, the better. I usually am too busy to do the planning. Keep it simple by inviting each family to contribute something to the party. If you don't ask for anything specific you may get drinks only, or if it turns out like my last party, ten different kinds of cupcakes. Request specific foods and party favors from different children. Assign two children forks and napkins, two children cut fruit and vegetables, two children cupcakes and drinks, and so on. This way, if one doesn't bring what you asked for, there is a chance the other did. I never require a child to bring a party food; the family might not be able to afford it, and donations are strictly voluntary. I let my room parent organize games like pin the tail on the donkey. If I don't have a room parent that year, I skip the games.

Teaching is difficult on party days. The students are usually excited, and it is challenging to get them to focus on academic work for more than a couple of hours. When their attention runs out, we write holiday stories, sing songs, read holiday books, watch festive movies, and do art projects. I like to think of class parties as a chance to appreciate and celebrate with all the children for their hard work and progress.

# A Crisis

During the process of writing this book the events of September 11 took place. On reflection I realized that I should include how to address a crisis in this survival guide. School remained open that day. The children arrived at school in the morning talking about what they had seen on the news. I had not been trained in handling this type of situation, so I went with my gut instinct, to talk about it and make sure every child understood that he or she was safe and protected at school. Here are a few things I've learned:

* Stay calm.
* Don't let the children know you are upset. Don't cry in front of them. Control your emotions. The children are carefully watching you to decide if they should be scared or feel safe.
* Let the students talk about what they know, have seen, and have heard.
* Answer their questions in a simple manner, leaving out the confusing or gory details.
* Speak only of the facts.
* Allow the children to express their feelings through talking, drawing, and writing.
* Assure them that they are in no danger.
* Continue with the school day as you had planned.
* Do something proactive. For example, my students wrote letters to other children who went to school close to ground zero.
* Watch your students carefully for signs of stress or fear and let the parents know of any concerns you have.

# Final Days of School

You've almost finished your first year of teaching. Hold on to your seat! You've got a lot to do. Excitement about the summer is building and you may be feeling like you are burned out. This is normal. Remember to pace yourself as you run the final mile of the academic

*The Primary Teacher's Survival Guide*

year marathon. Keep a list of things to do. Prioritize tasks. Breathe in. Breathe out. Everything will be completed on time.

## Paperwork

Anticipate paperwork. Some of the things you will have to make time for are presented here:

* Final report cards, your last grades and comments
* End of the school year testing: the amount of work required depends on your school district
* Student portfolio entries: in my district this includes test scores, protocols, and a scored writing sample
* Filling out information in each child's cumulative folder: usually includes gluing the child's school picture, writing what units the child was taught, the child's attitude toward school, parental involvement, and any special programs the student participated in
* Filling out student placement cards: these cards contain information for next year's teacher, such as their current reading level, math level, behavior issues, parent involvement, and level of English Language Fluency. These cards may be referred to when creating next year's classes to help ensure student diversity.
* Summer school referrals: my district has an academic jump-start summer school for students who need extra help and practice to be better prepared for the next grade. The paperwork includes writing about the child's strengths and weaknesses and copies of current test scores.

## Activities

Are your students becoming less and less attentive? Are some of the children acting out in ways you have never seen before? That's just how it is. At the end of the year I loosen up a little on behavior management. Remember to have compassion and empathy. It's not easy being in school so long for the kids either. Some of them love the summer and are looking forward to family trips and the freedom to play all day. For others, school is the best part of their lives. They have friends there, books, opportunities to learn, and a teacher who loves them. Their school life is better than their home life. For these children, summer vacation may be long, difficult, and lonely.

Don't plan to teach long division in the last couple of weeks. You'll only frustrate yourself. I recommend taking some time to review the skills you've taught throughout the year. This will help your students carry their learning through the summer and into the next grade level. Other end of the year activities are included here.

### Field Trips

Go to the park for a picnic lunch, visit the beach, go to a museum that will reinforce the unit you just taught them, and visit the fire station or the post office.

### Writing

There are probably a lot of people who have helped your students throughout the year. Ask your students to write them thank you notes. I like to ask my students to write me a letter telling me what they learned in my class, what they liked the best, and what they liked the least. You can also ask your students to write a letter to next year's class, telling them what to expect and look forward to learning.

### Art

Put out all your paper scraps and leftovers for the children to use up and create something new. Ask the students to create new self-portraits to show how they have changed compared with the portrait they created in the beginning of the year.

### Visit Classrooms

Visit the classrooms of the next grade up. You might want to arrange an activity to do with this class or bring student-made books and stories to share. Visit students in the next grade down or invite them to your classroom. Your students will take pride in giving younger children a tour of their classroom and showing them what they will learn.

### Clean Up

Let students take part in washing desks and chairs, putting away books, and taking their work down from the walls.

### Circle Time

I like to sit in a circle with the class and give everyone a chance to share what they loved about the school year and what they plan to do over the summer. I use it as a moment to be serious and tell them with all my heart how much I love and appreciate them.

### Have a Party

Make it simple and ask everyone to pitch in a couple dollars so you can order a few pizzas. Another fun party is for everyone to make their own ice cream sundae.

### Reflection

Take some time to reflect on your year. I recommend journal writing. If you have been keeping a journal all along, read through your entries. You have come a long way! What was successful? What was a failure? How will you do it differently next year? What was your proudest moment?

I like to take all my student's addresses home at the end of the year and send them a postcard over the summer, thanking them for being in my class, wishing them luck in the next grade, and reminding them to keep reading every day. This is a part of my reflection and it brings me closure on the school year.

# Final Thoughts

No teacher is prepared for everything. You never know what is going to happen in the world, in your life, and in your classroom. Remember to be flexible. Do your best. The second time around will be easier.

# How Do I Teach and Still Have a Life?

I found myself at my desk minutes before recess, papers strewn five inches deep. I was helping a student write a story, another child had a nose bleed, the office was trying to reach me on the intercom, two children were fighting in the class library, the rest of the kids were talking and not doing their work, and the lens had just popped out of my eyeglasses! It was hysterical, a Woody Allen comedy. I'm not exaggerating. Teaching couldn't be any more demanding in those moments. Yet one by one the tasks were completed, the recess bell rang, and I was alone to pop the lens back into my glasses. The busyness boiled down to a reasonable simmer, and I wondered how I had survived the morning.

This is the most important chapter in the book. The previous chapters were meant to get you started and answer your questions. This chapter is about how to keep going in the face of the many challenges you will encounter. I have not been teaching for very long, but have already seen three incredible teachers burn out and quit teaching altogether after two to three years.

What is the number one challenge? *Stress.*

I will be completely honest with you. Teaching is stressful, and the first year most of all. Lesson planning is like reinventing the wheel every day. Discipline evolves from your philosophy of learning and some trial and error until you find what works for you and your students. There are papers to grade, committees to serve on, meetings with parents, and on and on. At times in my first year I felt like I was swimming in an avalanche of duties and details I could never have foreseen. On bad days I felt like I had been buried and left for dead.

But there's hope. After all, I'm still here.

# *Benefits of Being Stress Free*

There are obvious benefits to being a stress-free teacher. You may feel more energetic, healthy, happy, and in control of your work. There are also some not so obvious benefits. When I am free of stress I notice I am more aware of what is happening in my classroom and more sensitive to the emotions and needs of my students. I am more likely to notice subtle reading improvements, a child becoming less shy, or a student who arrived at school feeling depressed. I notice that the children are more responsive to me and open to taking risks when I am relaxed. Being stress free also helps me reflect on my teaching practices. When I am not frantic or overwhelmed I can take a moment to think about how a lesson was successful or in need of improvement. I am more creative, thoughtful, and articulate. Most of all, I can take pleasure in the success of my students and appreciate their uniqueness.

Remember, you will not be effective as a teacher if you are tired, sick, stressed, and cranky. As dedicated as you are and as needy as your students may be, you come first.

## *Boundaries*

Set boundaries for yourself. One of mine is never to bring work home on a weeknight. I learned that when I did bring work home I never did it anyway. I'd drag my tote bag into the house and set it by the door where it remained untouched (if not accidentally kicked) until I left in the morning. One day I left school with so much work to do, my students asked me if I was going to San Diego! Another boundary is to leave work by 4:30 PM. I needed to set this rule to avoid heavy traffic while driving and circling my busy neighborhood for half an hour in my daily ritual quest for parking. Of course, there can be exceptions to this rule, and it is vital to be flexible. For instance, when there is a long staff meeting or back-to-school night I would stay late. What helped me was to have something to look forward to after work so I would leave on time. For example, having a nice dinner with my boyfriend, a prepaid yoga class, a movie date, or just a long, hot bath. Another boundary is to go to bed early. I am one of those people who need at least eight hours of sleep in order to function. I'm in bed by 9 PM and up at 5:15 AM so I can beat the morning traffic and get to the copy machine before there is a line. This schedule works for me because I'm a morning person. Knowing how and when you do your best work will help you create a schedule that works for you.

I recommend keeping a separate personal calendar. Everything I do during my work hours is written on my school calendar, and everything I do on my own time is written on my personal calendar. This helps me to separate my work life from my home life. Occasionally, both schedules overlap, but I make a concerted effort to keep them separate.

### Just Say, "No, thank you"

My final boundary is about knowing when to say, "No, thank you." Teachers are asked to serve on many committees throughout their careers. From School Site Council, to PTA, to literacy committees, to social committees. Talk to your administrator and coworkers about how many of these you are expected to serve on and if they are volunteer or paid positions. Be very careful not to join too many. You are busy enough as a first-year teacher. Having too many commitments piled on top of all your other duties and responsibilities is overwhelming. I recommend not agreeing to take on more than three extra positions your first year. Depending on the work involved, even that could be too much. It can be hard to say no to the principal, but it is also important not to overextend yourself, or you and your teaching will suffer. First-year teachers are already overextended because they have so much to do and learn.

### Working Weekends and Personal Time

During my first year of teaching I found myself working in my classroom every Saturday. I felt I had to go in and clean, catch up on paperwork, and plan for the week ahead. My biggest comfort was that I wasn't alone. Other new teachers were usually tucked away in their classrooms as well. What surprised me was the number of experienced teachers who came in on the weekend. Alas, a teacher's work is never done. But every subsequent year of teaching I worked less and less during the weekends. Now, after five years, I no longer go in on the weekend at all. I refuse!

I've learned to let go of the things that are undone to make time for my personal life. I ask myself what is more important: having two days to myself or grading papers? If the papers aren't graded or the homework isn't ready to go out on time, life will go on. As I write this I think of how controversial my advice might sound. I'm not saying one should let everything go and be a sloppy, unplanned, irresponsible teacher. Just know when to draw the line between work and home. In other words, don't turn down an invitation to the ballet because you have papers to grade. If all you have in your life is teaching, you will not have a rich and interesting background to share with your students.

Personal time might seem obvious as a necessity for teaching, but it is also easy to forget the obvious once you become buried by the avalanche. Spend time with your family, read a book (not a teaching book, with the exception of this one of course), go for a hike, get a massage, clean the house, or do something creative like painting or cooking a gourmet meal. Call a friend, exercise, go to a museum, listen to music, go to a religious service, meditate, take a workshop or class in something you usually don't have time for, or simply get some extra sleep.

## Relaxation During the School Day

It is also important to find time for yourself during the school day. One or two minutes here and there are all it takes to recharge. The key is self-awareness. Self-awareness is about noticing your thoughts and how your body feels. When I am aware of how I am feeling, I can relieve my stress before I feel overwhelmed. Sometimes I can be so engrossed in the activities at hand that I don't notice my shoulders tightening, my posture drooping, my breathing becoming shallow, or that I am thirsty or hungry. The longer I ignore my body and state of mind when under stress, the more likely I am to catch a cold or get a headache.

To begin noticing stress in your body, start by learning what it feels like to be completely relaxed. My yoga class was helpful in teaching me how to notice my body and relax, but you can also learn on your own. The following exercise can be done at any time of the day, but be careful, it is especially useful in helping me fall asleep. Also, you might want to try teaching it to your students to help them relax before they take the standardized tests.

Lie down on the floor or in bed on your back. You can put a pillow under your knees if you are uncomfortable in this position. Spread your legs and arms apart a few inches, palms up and toes gently falling to the side. Notice your breathing. Feel your chest rise and fall, feel the air passing through your nostrils. Bring your breathing to your diaphragm. Put one hand on your stomach and feel it rise as you slowly inhale and fall as you exhale. Breathe slowly. After a couple of minutes turn your attention to noticing the sounds around you. Listen to the sounds indoors such as a clock ticking and gradually listen further and further away from you. Be aware of the present moment. After a few minutes bring your attention to your feet. Imagine them feeling warm and relaxed. I like to silently repeat to myself, "My feet are relaxing, my feet are relaxing, my feet are warm, my feet are relaxed." Move on to your legs, torso, back, internal organs, hands, shoulders, neck, face, and scalp with the same relaxing words. Then finally relax your entire body: "My entire body is relaxing, my entire body is relaxing, my entire body is warm, my entire body is relaxed." By now you should be feeling deeply relaxed. Take a few minutes to notice how this feels. When you are ready, slowly and gently begin to move your arms, legs, and head and slowly sit up. Walk around to get your circulation going again and keep that deeply relaxed sensation in your mind.

Periodically throughout the school day take a moment to scan your body for tightness and stress. Remember how it felt to be completely relaxed. I try to do this right before school starts, at recess, lunch, and after school, but I can even do it at my desk while the students are working. If I find I am feeling stressed I can focus on breathing deeply and relaxing that part of my body that is feeling tight with the technique mentioned previously. It takes less than a minute.

Simple stretches can help with relieving stress as well. Just rotating the shoulders and head can loosen the grip of tension in seconds. Walking or other gentle exercises work too.

### Get out of the Classroom

It is often helpful to get out of the classroom on a break, even to leave the school campus and see some of the outside world. Teachers can easily become *tunnel visioned* with so much work to do. I sometimes feel like a mole, burrowed in my room and having no contact with the outside world. Occasionally I'll walk around the track with coworkers at lunchtime, or I'll walk over to the bay to look at the water. If you find yourself feeling mole-like, even a trip to the staff room can help. Hanging out with other teachers in an informal environment can relieve tension and remind you that you are not alone in feeling overwhelmed. Be careful, though. Avoid teachers with negative attitudes. Sometimes staff room discussions can make a teacher feel more stressed out. I find that if I am feeling extrasensitive, and my coworkers are talking about all the work they have to do or other problems they're having, I can feel even more overwhelmed. On those days I prefer to be alone in a quiet place. Sometimes I lie on the floor in my classroom with all the lights turned out.

## Slow Down

Slowing down is also helpful in staying calm. Remember, it is better to work smarter than harder. By slowing down I have more time to think about the tasks at hand and avoid making awkward mistakes. For example, I was rushing to copy the weekly homework packets so I could send them out on time, and after twenty minutes of photocopying the pages back-to-back I discovered that pages were upside down and in the wrong order, and one page was even missing. Had I slowed down for a moment I would have seen my error and not wasted so much time and paper.

## Teacher Survival Box

During my first year of teaching I created one of the most important tools I have. I read about the idea in a teacher magazine long ago: the teacher survival box. I found a nice large paper box from the craft store and painted it decoratively. The really fun part was filling it with survival gear. I keep it on my desk for easy access. It has helped me through some tough and stressful days when I felt like giving up.

To make your own survival box you need a large decorative box or a plain box you can decorate yourself. Fill it with things that are important to you, are inspirational, or help you relax. Here are some survival box items that have worked for me:

herbal teas
musical tapes
photos of loved ones
pictures from favorite vacations
letters from friends

Figure 7–1  Teacher survival box

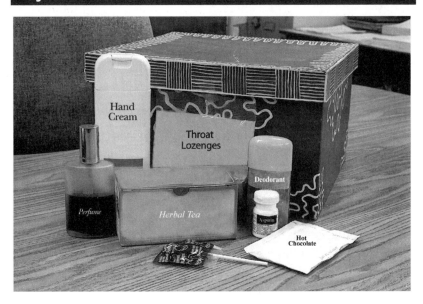

gifts and cards from students that say how much they love you
postcards and pictures of places you'd like to go
candy (especially chocolate)
ibuprofen
throat lozenges
foot roll for massaging your feet
journal
positive affirmations and prayers
poems
postcards of your favorite paintings
phone numbers of friends
deodorant (you never know when you might need extra)

If you plan to keep your survival box at home you might add some of the following items:

aromatherapy candles, spray, or perfume
incense
small bottle of wine

### Avoid Illness

Relieving stress is a major way to avoid illness while teaching. The less run down you are, the healthier you are. Working with kids exposes teachers to all kinds of bugs that make you sick. It is important to make time in your day for exercise and eating healthy foods, which will keep your energy up. I was amazed at how quickly I gained weight when I started teaching. Even though I was exhausted at the end of the day, I wasn't getting exercise. It has been a constant struggle to find time for a workout, but, whenever I do, I feel much more relaxed and healthy. You may have coworkers in the same predicament. Perhaps you can organize a group to exercise, diet, and join a health club together for mutual support and encouragement. Sports are a fun way to get exercise. So is biking, hiking, rollerblading, or taking a dance, a martial arts, or yoga class. Whatever it is, keep your body moving.

Use preventative measures to keep from getting sick. Wash your hands frequently; take vitamins; keep your hands away from your eyes, nose, and mouth; get a flu shot; drink lots of water; use disinfectant sprays on desks; and send home any child who is sick. Teachers are at risk for bladder and kidney infections because they often go for long periods of time without using the bathroom. Talk with the teacher whose classroom is closest to you. Ask the teacher if he wouldn't mind keeping an eye on your classroom from time to time so you can make a quick trip to the bathroom. You can return the favor.

When it comes to health, self-awareness is again the key. If I notice I'm feeling extra tired or I have a tickle in my throat, I know I need to slow down and take extra good care of myself. I get more sleep, pay special attention to eating right, and take my favorite home remedies like cold/flu tea with fresh lemon and ginger. Cold lozenges I get at the drugstore are excellent, too. I take them at the first sign of a cold and usually I do not get sick.

### Humor

Don't forget to laugh! I wouldn't have put a humorous story at the beginning of each chapter if a sense of humor wasn't an important skill for teaching. I find I feel better when I laugh at how crazy teaching can be. Even writing this book is stressful, but I have to laugh. The minute I started to write, the phone rang. It was a fax machine calling—wrong number! And it called again and again. I was having trouble concentrating, so I took the phone off the hook. Then the jack hammering started outside of my apartment. Then I couldn't get the toilet to stop running. Then my downstairs neighbors blasted their disco music. No, I am not kidding. I'm sure similar things happen to you as well. Obstacles are unavoidable. I try to remember to laugh in the face of chaos.

## Final Thoughts

Often the image comes to mind of an act I saw on the *Tonight Show* years ago. Carnival music was playing and a man came on stage who proceeded to spin thirty plates on sticks and attempted to keep them all from falling to the floor and breaking. He would run back and forth frantically to keep all the plates in the air. Occasionally, one would fall and he'd replace it with another plate. In the end he would collect the plates and take a bow as the audience applauded wildly. This act is not unlike some of the moments you will encounter when teaching. You may break a few plates, but you're only human. Applaud yourself. Not everyone can do your job as well as you.

# What Resources Do I Have?

It was one of those days, no, one of those months; I really wished my mom didn't live so far away. I couldn't help but think she would have fun helping me set up my classroom and especially shopping for supplies the week before school started. Every day I was out and about, buying plastic refillable ketchup bottles for glue, games for rainy days, crayons, folders, flash cards, or a doormat. I fantasized about giving mom the list and sending her on my scavenger hunt while I stayed back at school and scrubbed desks and set up bulletin boards.  It was a two-person job. I envied coworkers who had husbands, children, and other relatives and friends helping them every day. Inspiration and determination got me through that week. I was no ordinary average citizen, I was something more, and I was—Superwoman!

If your classroom is anything like mine as I described in Chapter 1, you will need a lot of classroom supplies. Just a few suggestions are listed in the next sections. Your coworkers are your greatest resource for local places to buy inexpensive supplies or even get some free. Ask them for help, especially if you are new to the area where your school is located.

Save all of your receipts. Several times I have used up all my supply money from the school, only to later receive an additional budget. I was able to submit the receipts I had saved and get reimbursed right away. You may also want to look into saving receipts for tax deductions.

# Inexpensive Supplies

* Check with your school secretary before buying any supplies. Find out if the school keeps some materials on hand such as pencils, tissue, writing paper, and construction paper. The school may also have a cheap source of supplies from catalogs.
* Discount stores like Wal-Mart and Target have big sales on school supplies in July and August. The prices are cheaper than most office supply catalogs the schools use.
* Your local teacher supply store probably has an annual sale around the time school starts. Though these stores can be expensive, you may find some good deals.
* Wholesale bookstore: There used to be a book warehouse here in the Bay Area that sold books to teachers at a discounted price. Finding one of these stores is like finding a goldmine. Check the Yellow Pages and ask other teachers if you have one in your area.
* At Costco, Priceclub, and other warehouse grocery stores you can find office supplies in bulk, discounted books, and snacks for your students.
* Garage sales and second-hand stores can be great for finding lamps, couches, books, electronics, and anything else you might need. I understand that you probably won't have time to check all the local garage sales, but keep your eyes open.
* Scrap stores: In the Bay Area I know of two stores that take donations of supplies from businesses and factories and sell them back to teachers and nonprofit organizations very cheaply. For example, I bought supply baskets for five cents apiece and bookends for twenty cents. You will find things like binders, paper, stamps, magnets, plastic milk caps (great as manipulatives), and stickers.
* Catalogs: If you have time to wait for your shipment, there are some school and office supply catalogs that offer incredible discounts.
* The World Wide Web: Some on-line catalogs offer the best discounts of all. If you have access to the Internet and time to browse, it can be worth the effort.
* Teacher discounts: Many stores offer teacher discounts from five to fifteen percent. It is always worth asking. Usually you need to show some sort of identification; I use my Union membership card or paycheck stub.

## Free

* Local libraries periodically clear out their shelves and offer older books for free. Call your library to find out when you can take advantage of this opportunity.
* Scholastic book orders: When your students order books, you are awarded bonus points. You can use these bonus points to order free books or other supplies from their catalog. I saved up enough points to order a small refrigerator and later a microwave.
* Grants: I have not written one myself, yet, but I know many teachers who have. In fact, some of my coworkers have been asked to assist in grant writing with the principal. It is a good skill to have. I recommend reading *I'll Grant You That* by Jim Burke and Carol Ann Prater (Heinemann, 2000) to help get you started. You might also try writing your first grant with a co-worker who has done it before, just to get your feet wet.

## Donations

* Parents: Parents are an excellent source of supplies. Create a list of things you need, go over the list with your students, and send it home. Please see the section on back-to-school night in Chapter 6, for ideas of what to write on your list.
* The wish list: My friend Craig Newmark, creator of craigslist.org, and Rick Karp, the owner of Cole Hardware, created a teacher wish list. You can go on-line, register your name and school, and then pick discounted items you need for your classroom from Cole Hardware's on-line catalog. Donors log on to the site, click on your name, and buy you the supplies you listed. The donors can use a credit card and their purchase is tax deductible. I've received many needed supplies. It is truly a blessing. The address is wishlist.craigslist.org.

## Other Tips

Don't throw anything away. You can recycle many materials to make arts and crafts projects. Create a recycling bag at home for milk cartons, plastic frosting and yogurt containers, toilet paper tubes, egg cartons, plastic caps and lids, packing peanuts, and wrapping paper tubes.

# Help and Support

Help and support is vital to your success as a new teacher to prevent you from feeling burned out and isolated. Though you may be the only adult in your classroom, you are definitely not alone.

## Coworkers

Your coworkers are your greatest resource. They are dealing with the same educational issues and know what it's like to be a new teacher. Like me, they have learned through experience the techniques, shortcuts, ideas, and activities needed to make more effective use of their time and to make learning more engaging for their students. I don't think I would still be teaching if it wasn't for the support and help of my fellow teachers.

## Buddy or Mentor

Ask your principal if a beginning teacher support program is available in your district. If so, I highly recommend participating. As a new teacher I participated in Beginning Teacher Support and Assessment for two years.

I was assigned a support teacher at my grade level in my school. We met once a week to discuss problems, questions, successes, and failures. I was given release time to observe her teaching lessons, and she came to my room to observe me and give me feedback. Every time I had a problem or was unsure of a procedure or policy, I could go to her for help. If there is no specific program, ask your principal for a buddy or support teacher, preferably at your grade level.

## Grade Level Teams

I cannot even begin to stress how important it is for teachers at the same grade level to work as a team. One of my best experiences in teaching has been going to grade level meetings once a week. As a new teacher, these meetings were especially helpful. Even though I had all the required teacher training, I wasn't sure what to do in the classroom. I sat down to my first meeting with my grade level team and was blown away. Everyone pulled out their lessons and activities for the month and shared them with each other. At the end I had everything I needed for the month of September, plus the wisdom of three experienced teachers.

*The Primary Teacher's Survival Guide*

Sharing and communication is key. At back-to-school night I tell the parents that I work closely with the other teachers at the same grade level. Their children have me and the best of my coworkers all rolled into one person. We work together to offer the very best education we can give. I hope your school has an atmosphere of teamwork and collaboration. If not, it can be difficult to bring about helpful changes. Ask your coworkers if they would be willing to meet with you one day after school to share ideas, discuss students you share, plan lessons, and possibly make your work easier. Perhaps not all the teachers at your grade level are interested in collaboration, but even one teacher can make a world of difference.

### *Benefits of Grade Level Collaboration*

* shared expertise and ideas
* grade level planning of curriculum and homework
* problem solving
* professional and emotional support
* discussing student progress
* creating rubrics for grading student work

## What Questions to Ask

There is a lot of information you need as a new teacher that I simply cannot give you. Every state, district, and school policy is slightly different. You need to ask questions. When I was a new teacher I didn't know what questions to ask because of my inexperience. The following section contains additional people resources and the many questions I have asked them over the years. Read through the section, highlight what you don't know, cross out the questions you already know the answers to, and add any queries you have of your own. Be careful not to flood any one person with too many questions. You may want to start with the ones that are most important to you. Don't forget to ask what you can do to make their job easier.

### Other Teachers

Other teachers at your school may also be eager to assist you. As you begin to get to know them, take a few minutes to visit them in their classrooms. Compliment them on the things you like, for example, a great bulletin board display. Always ask if you may borrow their ideas. Most teachers will be happy to share.

It is also important to discuss the curriculum with teachers at grade levels below and above your own. This gives you a better understanding of what your students should know when they come into your class and what they will need to know when they leave.

### Questions for Teachers

* Is there a PE, music, and/or art program, and what is the schedule?
* What are the duties and responsibilities of the secretary, and what can I depend on her to help me with?
* What are the playground rules that I need to enforce while on recess duty?
* Is there a policy for sending children to the bathroom during class time?
* Is there a schedule for school-wide events?
* What procedures should I follow when attending an assembly?
* What are the daily attendance procedures?
* Do I have email and how do I access it?
* Where do the students line up in the morning and at recess?
* Where do the busses load and unload?
* What are the lunch procedures?
* What are the field trip policies and procedures?
* Do I have all the textbooks and grade level–required materials to begin teaching the adopted curriculum?
* Where do I take my teaching materials to laminate?
* Is there a die cutter available?
* Does the district have a library of teaching materials for me to check out? How do I use it?
* Is there a kiln? How is it operated?
* Am I required to teach PE? Where do I find PE equipment?
* Who is the union representative? When and where are the local meetings?
* When and where do I get my paycheck?
* What are the district's language arts and math standards for my grade level?
* Are there any programs that bring classroom volunteers to my school?

* How do I check out books from the school library?
* Do I have a mailbox, and where is it located?
* Where should I park?
* Where is the lost and found?
* Where do I send children with injuries?
* What technology (digital camcorder, scanner) is available to me at the school?
* Does the school keep a student portfolio?
* What district and state assessments do I need to give this year, and what dates are they administered?
* How do I get a document translated into another language? Is there a translation policy?
* Do I have voice mail? How does it work?
* Who do I see about technology problems?
* How many committees am I required to volunteer for? What are my choices?
* How are bake sales handled?
* What is the procedure for picture day?

## Principal

The principal has a big job managing the entire school. The job can be very busy and stressful. But, all principals are different. They have different styles of handling problems, leadership, organization, and communication. During the first weeks of school, observe how your coworkers relate to her. Some principals are buddy-buddy with the staff; they frequently visit classrooms and get involved with what you're teaching. Others are more reserved and private to maintain their authority. It will take time to get a feel for whether you are welcome to walk into her office to chat or ask questions.  Don't be afraid to use her as a resource. I generally go to my principal for help with the bigger things like finding out if there is room in the school budget for purchasing phonics workbooks or getting permission to observe a coworker who is known for her outstanding writing lessons. The following are questions that the principal would be able to answer.

### Questions for the Principal

* What procedures do I take in the event of an earthquake, fire, tornado, etc.?

* Is there a policy about sending difficult children to the office?
* Is there a policy about entering the school to work on the weekends? Does the school have an alarm system? How can I get in?
* Is there a dress code for teachers?
* Is there a fire code for classroom arrangement and wall displays?
* Will the school or district pay for workshops?
* Am I expected to submit lesson plans to the principal?
* Do I have a classroom aide? Are there guidelines for the use of their time?
* When are staff meetings held? What do I need to bring or prepare for when I come to them?
* At what time am I required to be at school? What time can I leave?
* What are the new teacher evaluation policies? Will I be observed? When and by whom?
* What is the district's promotion/retention policy?
* How do I refer a child to a child study team (or student study team)?
* How do I refer a child to testing for a learning or physical disability?
* What is the school's enrollment? Mission statement? Profile? Parent involvement and support? Special programs and support?

## The Secretary

The secretary has many responsibilities and is almost always busy. She manages the office, answers the phone, sorts the mail, and in many schools patches up cuts and scrapes the children acquire on the playground. The secretary also knows school procedures and policies like the back of his hand and knows whom to call when he can't answer your questions.

### Questions for the Secretary

* What do I do with the student information packets when the students return them?
* How do I get supplies?
* Where do I get student names and addresses?
* Where are student files kept?
* Do I get a first aid kit, and, if so, where is it stored?

* How do I use the copy machine? Do I need a special code? Am I limited on the number of copies I can make? Do I need to buy my own paper?
* If I take a course for college units, what is the procedure for submitting these for an increase on the pay scale?
* Where do I refer parents who want a tutor for their child?
* Is there a policy on making personal phone calls from school?
* Will you take a personal phone message on occasion?
* What is the policy on the administration of medicine to students?
* Is there a speech therapist?
* Is there a student counselor?
* Is there a school nurse?
* What do I do if I suspect a student has lice or an illness?
* How do I handle large donations? (It could happen!)
* What is my classroom budget?
* When are student vision and hearing tested?
* How do I mail a school-related letter? Are stamps available?

## Custodial Staff

Get to know your custodian. I've heard it said that the custodian knows what is going on in the school better than anyone. I don't know if this is true, but they do get around to everyone's room and often have a friendly relationship with the students. It seemed that at least once a week I needed the help of the custodian during my first year of teaching. Custodians have a hard job. Always thank them for any extra work they do for you.

### Questions for the Custodian

* Where can I find a ladder, hammer, and screwdriver to borrow?
* Where can I find extra furniture?
* Can you help me move heavy things? Raise and lower desks?
* Should I consult you when I plan on making big changes to my classroom?
* Do you erase the chalkboards? Should I write *save* on anything I don't want erased?
* When is my classroom vacuumed, garbage collected, and paper towels restored?
* How do I put in a work order for classroom repairs?

* Are there any fire marshal concerns that I need to be aware of? Extension cords? Doorway clearing? Projects hanging from the ceiling? Fire retardant paper?

### Librarian

Your school librarian is another excellent resource. She can show you how to check out books, access teacher resources, and reserve books for your class. When my students were studying plants, I asked our librarian to reserve the plant books so my students could check them out.

### District Personnel

Other district personnel who are available to help you are nurses; psychologists; speech therapists; community workers; literacy, math, and science coaches; beginning teacher mentors; personnel assistants; payroll technicians; computer technicians; and special project leaders. They are usually easy to reach by phone and can answer your questions then or by appointment.

### Parents

The parents of your students can also provide support. Many like to spend time in their child's classroom and be involved with their learning. Parents can read to individual or small groups of children, listen to children read, help one or two children who are struggling with a subject like math, supervise a small group or learning center, copy papers, staple papers, cut out or trace pictures for art projects, put up bulletin boards, type letters, or file papers. The most important thing to remember is be prepared for the visit. If you ask a parent to come in and help, have the work ready for her to do. Otherwise your volunteer ends up sitting and watching your lesson with nothing to do all day.

## Be Thankful

Don't forget to say thank you to everyone who helps you. Acknowledge the hard work they do and let them know how appreciative you are. Keep on hand blank cards and stationary for these occasions. It only takes a minute to write a thank you note or thank them in person. Remember special days like Secretary's Day, the principal's birthday, and the custodian's birthday. Your students can practice being thankful too. Ask them to make cards, a poster, or an art project like tissue paper flowers for these occasions. Other times when you may want to say thanks are before winter vacation and before the last day of school. Have the children write letters to guest speakers, volunteers, and people who donate money or supplies to your classroom. Other thank you gifts include tote bags and T-shirts signed by the students in fabric paint; class photos transferred to tote bags, T-shirts, mugs, or calendars; spiral-bound student letters; flowers, books, and gift certificates.

## *Final Thoughts*

There may be times when you feel alone and isolated in your job. This is only an illusion. It takes many people to smoothly run a school and meet the needs of the children. Someone is always there to help; all you need to do is ask.

# Epilogue

As I read through the pages in this book it all sounds so easy. If I didn't know myself so well I would think I'm an expert at teaching and never have problems or a bad day. But that's not true. Teaching is always full of challenges. However, it does get easier.

## How Long Does It Take to Know What You're Doing?

It wasn't until my third year that I started relaxing into the job. By my fifth year I actually started to feel confident. There are still new situations that arise, new students, grade level changes, school changes, classroom moves, new administrators, new curricula to learn, and new world events to explain and interpret. Nothing in education ever stays the same.

# Reflecting on Your Teaching

You are now a professional. Good teaching practice means reflecting on your work. Think about how your day went. What went well in your lessons? What did not work as you had planned? Why? What can you do differently next time? This kind of reflection and questioning doesn't just apply to your lessons. What about how you handled a behavior issue, a disagreement with a coworker or administrator, or a parent who asked you for help and advice?

Pick an area of teaching you want to improve on and focus on that for a few months, or perhaps a year. You might want to spend a year focusing on classroom discipline, learning environment, or assessment.

Video tape yourself. You don't have to show it to anyone. Watch it yourself in the privacy of your own home. What do you look like when you are teaching? How do you come across to your students? Do you have any distracting habits? How many times do you say "um" in an hour?

# Learning from Your Students

Your students have a lot to teach you. If you tried a new teaching technique and their faces are glowing with excitement and success, use that strategy in other areas. If your students are confused and having difficulty with an assignment, try a different approach. Ask the children what they need to better learn a skill. What they have to say will surprise you.

# Professional Development

The professional teacher is always looking for ways to improve, learn new things, and grow. Take advantage of any workshops your district has to offer or go on your own during weekends or vacations. Read professional books, journals, and magazines. Maybe even go back to school part time for a second degree. Here are some books I couldn't teach without:

### Language Arts

*Spelling Through Phonics* by Marlene J. McCracken and Robert A. McCracken, Peguis Publishers Limited, 1982
*Making Words* by Patricia M. Cunningham and Dorothy P. Hall, Good Apple, 1994
*Guided Reading, Good First Teaching for All Children* by Irene C. Fountas and Gay Su Pinnell, Heinemann, 1994
*Invitations, Changing as Teachers and Learners K–12* by Regie Routman, Heinemann, 1991
*…And with a Light Touch, Learning about Reading, Writing, and Teaching with First Graders, First Edition* by Carol Avery, Heinemann, 1993
*75 Creative Ways to Publish Students' Writing* by Cherlyn Sunflower, Scholastic Inc., 1993

### Math

*Box It or Bag It Mathematics Teachers Resource Guide for First-Second* by Donna Burk, Allyn Snyder, and Paula Symonds, The Math Learning Center, 1988
*Quilting Through the Year, a Collection of Primary Quilts* by Paula Symonds, A Teaching Resource Center Publication, 1999

*About Teaching Mathematics a K–8 Resource* by Marilyn Burns, Math Solutions Publications, 1992
*A Collection of Math Lessons from Grades 1 Through 3* by Marilyn Burns and Bonnie Tank, Math Solutions Publications, 1988

### Science

*The California State Environmental Education Guide* by Carolie Sly, Leslie Comnes, and Celia Cuomo, Alameda County Office of Education, 1988

### Art

*Drawing with Children* by Mona Brooks and Jeremy P. Tarcher, Perigee Books, 1986

### Miscellaneous

*Mosaic of Thought, Teaching Comprehension in a Reader's Workshop* by Ellin Oliver Keene and Susan Zimmermann, Heinemann, 1997
*Tribes, a Process for Social Development and Cooperative Learning* by Jeanne Gibbs, Center Source Publications, 1987
*The Pre-Referral Intervention Manual, the Most Common Learning and Behavior Problems Encountered in the Educational Environment* by Stephen B. McCarney, Hawthorne, 1988
*The Teacher's Book of Lists* by Sheila Madsen and Bette Gould, Good Year Books, 1994
*How is My First Grader Doing in School?* by Jennifer Richard Jacobson, Fireside, 1998 (other grade levels are also available)

### Discipline

*Assertive Discipline, Positive Behavior Management for Today's Classroom* by Lee Canter and Marlene Canter, Lee Canter and Associates, 1992

*Parents on Your Side, a Comprehensive Parent Involvement Program for Teachers* by Lee Canter and Marlene Canter, Lee Canter and Associates, 1991

### Computer Programs

DJ Inkers, clip art and fonts

Your professional development doesn't necessarily have to have to deal specifically with teaching. I am always enrolling in an art class or naturalist workshop. Be a student yourself. Bring back what you learned to your classroom. I am going to share the process of writing this book with my students. From my experience and example I can teach them what goes into writing a book, explain how many drafts my work went through, and how challenging it was at times.

# Hopes, Fears, and Reality

One of the biggest mistakes I see first-year teachers make is setting their expectations too high. After going through teacher training, student teaching, and observing mentor teachers I had a fairly clear idea of what an effective classroom environment and teaching should look like. I fell into the trap of thinking that this is what my classroom would be like when I started teaching. The reality is this: Dream classrooms are not built in a day. The mentor teachers I observed had spent years perfecting their craft and inventing all their clever tools. Yes, I wanted that wisdom in place the moment I began teaching, but when I started working on all the elaborate bulletin boards, customized literacy centers, and individualized homework, the reality set in. It would be years before my classroom started to look and function the way I really wanted it.

# The Joy of Teaching

Lastly, take some time to appreciate the joy of teaching. You are bringing your love of learning, knowledge, diversity, creativity, curiosity about the world we live in, stability, compassion, and love into the lives of your students. These children are our future. Even one awesome teacher can make a difference in the life of a child. The smallest gestures can make a difference. Just the fact that you are in your classroom every day, consistent in your attendance, can give a student a sense of stability and consistency. I was lucky to have two awesome teachers. Both made me feel good about myself—special, smart, talented, like I could do anything. That's how I want my students to feel. It is a gift that lasts a lifetime.

# Index